# From Liberty to Tyranny

## How Expansion, Warfare, Economic Crisis, and Entitlements Threaten Personal Liberty in the United States

**Abraham Thornton**

# Contents

# Preface

# Reflections on a Nation Gone Mad

*"What has always made the state a hell on earth has been precisely that man has tried to make it his heaven"*
Johann Hölderlin

In May of 2011, the Federal government of the United States hit its debt ceiling, the total amount of debt allowed it by law. At that particular moment, the debt ceiling was at $14,294,000,000,000. To put this in perspective, the Gross Domestic Product (GDP) for the United States was $14.12 trillion in 2009. This means that if the total value of every good and service produced for a full year in the world's largest economy (the European Union is not counted here, as it is not a country, but a group of countries) were 100% dedicated to debt reduction, the United States would still have a credit card balance of over $100 billion dollars.

After weeks of the two ruling parties in the U.S. Congress making a big show over playing hardball with each other, which included some of the most dishonest pandering and emotional appeals in political history, both sides apparently got tired of taking the American public for a ride and reached an inevitable agreement that increased the debt ceiling to $15 trillion in exchange for what turned out to be around $38 billion, or 1% of the annual federal budget, in spending cuts.

This increase in the nation's credit card limit didn't last long; the $15 trillion limit was hit in November of 2011, meaning that the U.S. government managed to rack up nearly $800 billion in debt in a matter of 6 months. At the time that the debt ceiling was hit, government was borrowing at the rate of $4 billion per day, and has projected deficits of more than $1 trillion per year for the foreseeable future.

Where does all of the money go? Most is spent on entitlement programs; the combination of Medicare and Medicaid cost the United States $793 billion in 2010, and Social Security payments totaled $701 billion. Together, these programs represented 43% of the 2010 federal budget. The defense department, including the military operations in Iraq and Afghanistan and the approximately 1,000 bases being operated on foreign soil, consumed $689 billion in 2010, making it the third-largest component of the federal budget, and representing nearly half of global military expenditures. This madness cannot continue; Standard and Poor, one of the world's largest credit-rating agencies, has already downgraded U.S. credit, and China, one of the United States' largest debt holders, began divesting itself of U.S. debt in 2011[1].

In addition to crippling debt, individual liberty is at its lowest level in American history. The economic freedom

---

[1] As Reported in CNS News, June 3, 2011

rating of the United States, as measured by the Heritage Foundation, continues to slide, and will likely leave the top ten within the next few years[2]. Reporters Without Borders, which ranks press freedom annually, ranked the United States 47th in press freedom in their 2011-2012 assessment[3] . For a nation that was founded with the intention of being the freest society in the world, this is an embarrassment. Economic liberty is not the only liberty in decline; Americans are subject to over 150,000 pages of federal regulations, dealing with everything from the construction of baby cribs, to the operation of tractors on family farms, to the amount of water their toilets and showerheads use. There is literally nothing that the federal government does not believe that it has the authority to regulate about your business or your private life.

Any student of American history knows that this is not the way things were supposed to be. The architects of the Declaration of Independence and the American Revolution originally set the nation up as a loose association of autonomous states, which were united for the purpose of common defense and economic development. Thomas Jefferson, who penned the Declaration, spent not only his public life, but his private life following retirement, arguing against government authority and in favor of a political system that today would be considered extremely libertarian. The overall mood of the Revolutionaries was possibly best summed up by Thomas Paine, who opined that "Society in every state is a blessing, but Government, even in its best state, is but a necessary evil; in its worst state, an intolerable one." In the minds of these men, the only proper purpose of

---

[2] According to the Heritage Foundation 2012 rankings

[3] Reporters Without Borders 2011/2012 Press Freedom Index

government was to protect life and private property, allowing men the freedom to do whatever they wished, provided that those urges did not infringe upon the similar freedoms of his neighbors.

This sentiment was not universal, however. There were men, such as Alexander Hamilton, who almost immediately advocated for a strong central government. As libertarian as Jefferson's ideals were, Hamilton's were just as authoritarian. In fact, given Hamilton's philosophy on government, it is hard to believe that he risked life and limb to fight against the British monarchy, which appears to have all the hallmarks of what Hamilton considered good government. As members of Washington's cabinet, Jefferson and Hamilton would frequently and passionately disagree. To this day, a bust of Hamilton adorns a pedestal in the foyer at Jefferson's Monticello; it is speculated that it was placed there as a conversation starter, so that Jefferson could regale his visitors with expositions on how wrong Hamilton was.

The debate on the proper role of government has been part of America since the beginning, and while the United States may have started with principles closer to those of Jefferson, the current role that the federal government occupies is far more in line with Hamilton's vision. Given the financial situation that the nation is in, perhaps we have a final verdict on whose philosophy was correct.

In 1944, following Europe's descent into socialist authoritarianism, and in the midst of America's transformation under the leadership of Franklin Roosevelt, economist F.A. Hayek warned of the dangers of a centrally-planned economy. In *The Road to Serfdom*, the case is made that central planning will necessarily lead to a loss of liberty, as central planners build a nation's economy around a 'bigger picture' instead of allowing market forces to direct its trajectory. He also makes the case that any centrally-planned economy will fail to accomplish the goal of a 'greater good' because all men have different definitions of good. The 'greater good' then becomes the good as defined by those in charge, not the nation as a whole. In Hayek's own words:

> "The 'social goal' or 'common purpose' for which society is to be organized is usually vaguely described as the 'common good,' the 'general welfare,' or the 'general interest.' It does not need much reflection to see that these terms have no sufficiently definite meaning to determine a particular course of action. The welfare and the happiness of millions cannot be measured on a single scale of less and more. The welfare of a people, like the happiness of a man, depends on a great many things that can be provided in an infinite variety of combinations. It cannot be adequately expressed as a single end, but only as a hierarchy of ends, a comprehensive scale of values in which every need of every person is given its place."

The attempt to plan for the 'greater good' of millions will necessarily result in the planner's choosing of one man's definition of 'good' over another's. This is the very definition of totalitarianism; one man's destiny is determined by another in a superior position.

Any attempt to maximize the winners through central planning will also be met with disaster. The more people that a central authority tries to serve, the more complex the plan becomes, and since definitions of 'greater good' differ from man to man, those ends will necessarily become contradictory, resulting in a massive bureaucracy that is often redundant and frequently contradictory in its goals.

When viewed this way, it becomes clear that not only does government centralization result in a loss of liberty; our suffocating regulations and entitlement programs have over-burdened our economy to the point where we are drowning in debt. Reasonable debt, by itself, is not a bad thing. In *Common Sense*, founding father Thomas Paine argues that the debt incurred to properly staff and equip an army sufficient to defeat the British occupation would be a good thing for the Colonies, as it would form a bond between the states. However, Paine also envisioned a libertarian society unencumbered by governmental regulation, and the fortune such a society reaps makes for easy payback on such a debt[4].

This is not the situation today, however. We have become a nation that wants things handed to us, and we expect our ever-expanding federal government to supply those wants while making us feel safe and secure. This combination of handouts and restrictions has stifled growth and resulted in a fiscal situation that is unsustainable, and an individual lifestyle completely removed from that which the founders of the United States envisioned.

As with any crisis, it is instructive to see how and where things all began, and try to determine where they all went wrong. This journey begins in 1776, and takes us all the way through to 2011, with stops along the way to see where the federal government has overstepped its legal authority, and how that overstepping has resulted in a nation that is less free and less financially stable.

---

[4] Numerous public-domain copies are available for free online. No specific edition is endorsed in this book.

When the entire history of the United States is looked at with an eye to determine what happened to move it from libertarian federal republic to authoritarian socialist state, there are five primary periods that stand out. The adoption of the Constitution set up a strong federal government with a strong executive, and while it also set up a clear balance of power to prevent abuse, subsequent generations have ignored those protections, allowing the Constitution itself to set the stage for the problems to come. Westward expansion, which grew out of the almost religious belief in manifest destiny, began the shift from state to federal authority. The Civil War effectively ended state sovereignty and cemented federal supremacy. The Progressive Era set the federal government up as supreme not only over the states, but over the lives of individuals, and began the shift of power from a three-branch balance to the executive. The New Deal completed that shift, and also gave birth to the idea of the federal government as not only authority, but provider.

Through these five periods, the nation was fundamentally changed, and not for the better. The loss of liberty and crippling debt currently faced by the United States are a testament to this fact.

# One

# Founding Principles and Structure

*"My reading of history convinces me that most bad government results from too much government."*
Thomas Jefferson

In 1783, the British crown officially relinquished control of its territory east of the Mississippi river and south of the Great Lakes to a band of treasonous secessionists from the New World colonies. For eight years, the unifying factor for the rebels in the thirteen colonies had been the defeat of the British, but now the American Revolution was officially over, and its architects had the task of transitioning from a fight for independence to administering a new government.

This task had actually begun in earnest in 1776, when a committee established by the Second Continental Congress set to work on what was titled 'The Articles of

Confederation and Perpetual Union' – a document that was to become the first constitution of the United States of America. This founding document would officially be ratified in 1781, and would be in effect until the current Constitution replaced it in 1789. In the Declaration of Independence, writer Thomas Jefferson asserted that the Colonists were justified in their desire for separation and self-governance, and outlined the reasons that the Colonies had for dissolving their ties with Great Britain. In so doing, Jefferson provides at least a partial list of behaviors that any new government founded by the Colonies must not engage in; for to repeat these behaviors would be a violation of the very justification for secession. While to modern readers the Declaration may seem a radical document for its time, which breaks new political ground, the ideas that influenced the founding generation were nearly a century old by the time the Continental Congress convened in 1776.

In order to understand the founding principles of the United States, it is necessary to go back to the seventeenth century, and the writings of British political philosopher John Locke. Locke's revolutionary ideas on politics and governance, published in 1689 as *Two Treatises of Government*, heavily influenced many of the founders. In fact, the famous line from the Declaration of Independence, "We hold these truths to be self-evident, that all men are created equal, that they are endowed by their Creator with certain unalienable Rights, that among these are Life, Liberty and the pursuit of Happiness," is actually a modified version of Locke's claim that government cannot rightfully deny a man's natural right to "Life, Health, Liberty, or Possessions." Locke was so great an influence on Jefferson that the future President would write in a 1789 letter to artist John Trumbull, "I consider them (Francis Bacon, John Locke, and Isaac Newton) as the three greatest men that have ever lived, without any exception, and as having laid the foundations of those superstructures which have been raised in the Physical & Moral sciences."[5]

In his political works, Locke argues that the most natural state of man is complete liberty, and using this as a foundational position, builds the idea of legitimate government as one that protects this natural state. From *Two Treatises of Government*[6]:

> "To understand political power right, and derive it from its original, we must consider, what state all men are naturally in, and that is, a state of perfect freedom to order their actions, and dispose of their possessions and persons, as they think fit, within the bounds of the law of nature, without asking leave, or depending upon the will of any other man."

To Locke, and by extension the founders of the United States, liberty meant the ability for men to do as they pleased, and to enjoy the fruits of their labor without fear of confiscation. Locke also wrote about the immorality of free men being subjected to the whims of a ruling class:

> "...for men being all the workmanship of one omnipotent, and infinitely wise maker; all the servants of one sovereign master, sent into the

---

[5] Transcripts of this letter are available in many locations. For one such example, visit the Library of Congress at
http://www.loc.gov/exhibits/jefferson/18.html
[6] As with *Common Sense,* numerous public domain editions are available, both electronically, and in print.

world by his order, and about his business; they are his property, whose workmanship they are, made to last during his, not one another's pleasure: and being furnished with like faculties, sharing all in one community of nature, there cannot be supposed any such subordination among us, that may authorize us to destroy one another, as if we were made for one another's uses, as the inferior ranks of creatures are for ours."

All men, bearing the image of their Creator, are equal, and it is contrary to the laws of nature for a man to subjugate another. This viewpoint, which puts liberty above all other concerns, demands a very specific government. The founders' worldview was one in which life and private property were absolutes; indeed, one of the grievances outlined in the Declaration of Independence was that of taxation without consent, which men like Jefferson viewed as a theft of private property. In fact, most of the founders believed that the *only* legitimate purpose of government was to protect life and private property. In *Common Sense,* Thomas Paine outlines this particular line of thinking:

"Here then is the origin and rise of government; namely, a mode rendered necessary by the inability of moral virtue to govern the world; here too is the design and end of government, viz. freedom and security. And however our eyes may be dazzled with show, or our ears deceived by sound; however prejudice may warp our wills, or interest darken our understanding, the simple voice of nature and of reason will say, it is right."

Any attempt to provide an accounting for the United States and its history without acknowledging these core principles ignores the fundamental truth of the American experiment: that man is a free agent, and ought to be allowed to enjoy and use the fruits of his labor in whatever matter he sees fit, and be free from the intrusive efforts of other men. Government's legitimate role is to ensure the protection of life and private property; any other effort on its part is a violation of man's rightful state. It is in this context that the foundational structure of the United States must be viewed.

### *The Articles of Confederation and Perpetual Union*

In 1776, in the Pennsylvania State House, the Second Continental Congress would agree on two things that would change the course of history. First, the thirteen colonies represented in the Congress would pursue independence from Great Britain, and second, the new confederation would need a government. The first item would be embodied in the Declaration of Independence, a document which served as a formal notice of secession from the empire of Great Britain. In order to accomplish the second item, a committee was established by the Congress, with the purpose of drafting a national constitution. In 1777, the document, entitled "The Articles of Confederation and Perpetual Union" was completed and submitted to the states for ratification.

The Articles of Confederation contains many of the same enumerated powers that the current Constitution contains, but the structure of the government was very different. There was no Executive Branch, no Judiciary, and the Legislative branch consisted of a single house known as Congress. Each state was allowed a delegation of between two and seven members, but each state, regardless of population or delegation size, received one vote. The method for choosing state delegates was left to the states, and each state was required to pay for their own delegation. The primary powers of the Congress of the United States were the power to declare war, ratify treaties with other nations, appoint ambassadors, set the value of money and of weights and measures, and to settle land disputes between states. All of these powers required the approval of nine states, rather than the simple majority that we are accustomed to today. Perhaps the most drastic difference from our current system was that Congress lacked any authority to directly tax any citizen or corporation; all income was collected from the state governments based on the value of land and improvements in each state. This was not a problem for the government of the time; there was no provision for an executive branch, which today consumes the vast majority of the federal budget via its myriad bureaucracies. There was also no provision for a standing Army or Navy beyond what Congress deemed necessary for the protection of each state, and each state was responsible for funding its own defensive force.

The Articles of Confederation were different from our current federal government in one other important way: there was no direct input from the population at large. Since there was no executive, and the single-house Congress was made up of delegations chosen by the states, individual citizens effectively had no say in the decisions or policies of the federal government. In today's society, such a thought is almost unimaginable, and the likely reaction of most Americans when presented with a governmental model that does not allow the average citizen to vote is that such a society must live under tyranny; however, the opposite is true. Under the Articles of Confederation, the average citizen could not vote on the direction of the federal government, but it must also be understood that the federal government's activities had no bearing on the day-to-day life of the average citizen. The Congress had no authority to act on domestic issues; each state made their own laws on everything that did not relate to foreign affairs. The tendency to equate voting rights with liberty is a later convention, and one which, when the Progressive Era is discussed, will be shown to be not only false, but a dishonest trick often employed by political elites to curtail liberty. The truth is, there is far more liberty in a society where the government has so little authority that there is nothing to vote on than one in which the average citizen feels compelled to go to the polls every two years and hope that his fellow citizen does not decide to vote his rights away. Benjamin Franklin, discussing the ability for the population to vote on all manner of governmental affairs, put it thusly: "When the people find that they can vote themselves money, that will herald the end of the republic." The fact that the population has done just that, in the form of entitlements such as Social Security and Medicare/Medicaid, subsidized unemployment insurance, subsidized student loans, farm subsidies, corporate welfare, and myriad other giveaways, effectively proves Franklin's point.

The Articles were obviously severely limited, but the designers of the confederation considered this a feature, not a bug. Having just fought a bloody revolution against what they considered to be immoral abuses of executive power, and guided by the principles set forth by Locke, a weak central authority with no chief executive seemed the proper structure. As Thomas Jefferson would later write, "I would rather be exposed to the inconveniences attending too much liberty than those attending too small a degree of it." It was obvious to the framers that government was necessary in order to prevent man's wickedness from violating the liberties of the population, but it was also obvious that government would be made up of the same wicked men, and wicked men with the power of government behind them are a greater threat than wicked men left to their own devices. Thomas Paine put it this way:

> "Society in every state is a blessing, but government even in its best state is but a necessary evil; in its worst state an intolerable one; for when we suffer, or are exposed to the same miseries BY A GOVERNMENT, which we might expect in a country WITHOUT GOVERNMENT, our calamity is heightened by reflecting that we furnish the means by which we suffer."

It would not be long, however, before the Articles came under attack from those who favored a stronger central authority. In fact, in May of 1787, less than a decade after the Articles of Confederation were ratified, a convention was called to address the weak nature of the federal government. The primary complaints against the Articles were:

*Failure to Support an Army:* While the Congress had the authority to command the combined state militias, and could place requests for troops and requisition equipment, it had no power either to draft troops or compel industry to provide supplies. Federalist critics of the Articles pointed to the long, starving winters suffered by Revolutionary troops, along with reluctance for states to send troops when fighting was far from their borders, as a reason to strengthen the federal government.

*Weakness in Foreign Policy:* Following the end of the Revolutionary War, the British agreed to vacate forts it had occupied in the western frontier, which was now technically part of the United States. However, it violated that agreement and kept the forts staffed. The government lacked the diplomatic power to force them out. Additionally, the inability of the Congress to raise funds left the United States without a Navy, making merchant shipping vulnerable to the Barbary Pirates, who operated off of the coast of North Africa. Even Thomas Jefferson, a critic of a strong federal government, was frustrated by the failure to raise a navy, writing "It will be said there is no money in the treasury. There never will be money in the treasury till the Confederacy shows its teeth. The states must see the rod." Given that Jefferson was extremely hostile to strong centralized government, this demonstrates that the Articles of Confederation did have some serious flaws, particularly the inability of the national government to raise any kind of revenue to support its limited mandate.

*No Power of Taxation:* The federal government relied on state governments for its funding. This funding was to be based on the value of land and infrastructure in the state, similar to modern property taxes. Congress could not directly tax individuals or businesses, and had no real power to force states to pay their share. States frequently ignored their funding obligations, resulting in a tremendous cash shortfall for the fledgling nation.

The Constitutional Convention, which took place in the same Philadelphia statehouse where the Declaration of Independence and the Articles of Confederation were drafted, would expose a rift between two opposing groups of founders: those who saw a weak federal government as the only way to preserve liberty, and those who favored a stronger central authority. The Federalists, who favored strengthening the federal government, were led by James Madison and Alexander Hamilton. Their opposition, creatively dubbed the Anti-Federalists, included Patrick Henry, Samuel Adams, and George Mason, among others. Thomas Jefferson, living abroad in Paris at the time, was not considered a key Anti-Federalist, although he made it clear that his allegiance was with those who worked against strengthening federal authority. Looking back, it was perhaps Patrick Henry who had the best way to articulate what was to come. He boycotted the convention, stating that he "smelt a rat in Philadelphia, tending toward the monarchy." Two hundred and twenty-four years later, with the size and scope of the executive branch what it is, the only logical conclusion is that Henry was correct.

### *The Constitution – A Step Back Toward Monarchy*

Originally billed as a meeting to discuss modifications to the Articles of Confederation, it quickly became obvious that those in charge of the Pennsylvania Convention of 1787 had every intention of replacing, not repairing, the articles. A number of options were put on the table for discussion which ranged from the New Jersey plan, which created a bicameral legislature and an executive branch and granted the authority to levy taxes, but not much else, to the radical Hamilton Plan, proposed by Alexander Hamilton, which completely eliminated state sovereignty in favor of a single unified government consisting of a bicameral legislature and an executive. Both the chief executive, termed the Governor, and members of the Upper House of the legislature would be chosen by electors for a life term. For a nation that had only four years earlier claimed victory against an overbearing monarch, it is astounding that a plan like Hamilton's would even be considered, and shows just how quickly the ideals of liberty are abandoned in favor of submission to a consolidated power.

The final structure agreed to during the convention, and outlined in the new Constitution, contained a bicameral legislature; the Lower House to have seats appointed to each state based on population and members determined by popular vote, and the Upper House to have a fixed number of two seats apportioned to each state, regardless of population, to be appointed by the state legislature (direct election of Senators would replace legislative appointment in 1913 with the ratification of the seventeenth amendment). The Constitution also established two new branches of the federal government: the Executive, to be led by a President elected to a four year term, and a Judiciary, the members of which would be appointed by the President and confirmed by the Senate for a life term. The purpose of the executive branch was to ensure enforcement of laws passed by the Legislature, to serve as the nation's chief diplomat, and to prosecute wars declared by Congress. The purpose of the Judiciary was to ensure that the rule of law was equally and properly applied in all areas in the federal government's jurisdiction. Additionally, the power to levy taxes was granted to the legislature, guaranteeing the federal government a source of revenue.

This new Constitution resulted in a much stronger central government than was seen under the Articles of Confederation; specifically, the existence of a chief executive was a matter of much concern for people who feared that they were seeing the creation of a monarchy.

The Federalists, however, argued that the strong central authority was necessary for building and maintaining a strong country. In direct contradiction to the ideas of Locke, who argued that natural law was the only governance that man needed, John Jay argued in *Federalist Number 2* that man must, by necessity, cede his liberty to government[7]:

> "Nothing is more certain than the indispensable necessity of government, and it is equally undeniable, that whenever and however it is instituted, the people must cede to it some of their natural rights in order to vest it with requisite powers."

Breaking with Jefferson and Paine, who insisted that government was a "necessary evil" and that Natural Law should govern men, Jay instead claimed that government is indispensable, and that man should willfully surrender his God-given rights to government, that it may have the power necessary to do its work.

The primary work that Jay discusses in *Federalist Number 2* is that of domestic security. The United States had defeated the world's most formidable military just four years earlier, but Jay argues that the great military powers of Europe would not sit idly by while the upstart colonies assert and exercise their independence. According to Jay, it was only a matter of time before Britain, France, or some other European power would attempt to re-colonize the region; the only proper defense against such an invasion would be to give up rights to a central authority to ensure security. In 2011, as air travelers endure the groping of their genitalia (or the genitalia of their children) by federal

---

[7] The *Federalist Papers* are also available as public domain material, in various formats.

agents in the name of security, it is clear that such appeals work, and lead to the worst kind of abuses by those in power.

## Negative Reception

When the Constitution was submitted to the states for ratification, the reception was hardly warm. State legislatures viewed the drastic strengthening of the federal government as a threat to their sovereignty, and individual citizens were wary of what they viewed as a king-like figure. Although eleven of the states would eventually ratify the constitution, there were holdouts. North Carolina refused to ratify until the document was amended to include a bill of rights. Several other states, including Virginia, signed without the bill of rights, although they demanded that one be included, and specified in their ratification document that they possessed the authority to withdraw from the Union should the federal government overstep its authority. Seventy years later, they would learn that the new national government had no intention of honoring that requirement. Rhode Island, which had completely boycotted the convention, flat-out refused to ratify; their acceptance of the new government would come in 1790, a year after George Washington took office, and it nearly resulted in a civil war. It should be noted that the ratification process itself was a violation of the agreement in the Articles of Confederation, which required unanimous agreement to either modify or abandon the Articles (hence the 'Perpetual Union'); Rhode Island's refusal to ratify the Constitution should have put a legal block on implementation of the new government, and shows that governmental breach of contract has been with the United States from the beginning.

## *The Bill of Rights*

One of the requirements many states placed on the new constitution was that a bill of rights be amended to the document in order to restrict federal power. They feared the authority of a centralized government, and sought to secure some key protections for themselves and their citizens. From the minutes of the Virginia ratification convention[8]:

> "MR. Wythe reported, from the Committee appointed, such amendments to the proposed Constitution of Government for the United States, as were by them deemed necessary to be recommended to the consideration of the Congress which shall first assemble under the said Constitution, to be acted upon according to the mode prescribed in the fifth article thereof; and he read the same in his place, and afterwards delivered them in at the clerk's table, where the same were again read, and are as followeth: That there be a Declaration or Bill of Rights asserting and securing from encroachment the essential and unalienable rights of the people in some such manner..."

Although Virginia ratified the Constitution without a bill of rights, and merely requested one be adopted upon the first meeting of the new Congress, Virginia delegate George Mason refused to sign the Constitution during the convention because it lacked such a bill.

Not surprisingly, the Federalists argued against a bill of rights, while the anti-Federalists argued that it was

---

[8] From the U.S. Constitution online:
http://www.usconstitution.net/rat_va.html

the minimum requirement for restraining a strong federal government such as the one that the Constitution outlined. According to Thomas Jefferson, "A Bill of Rights is what the people are entitled to against every government, and what no just government should refuse, or rest on inference." It seems that inference, however, was just what Constitutional author Alexander Hamilton had in mind. In Hamilton's own words[9]:

> "I go further, and affirm that bills of rights, in the sense and in the extent in which they are contended for, are not only unnecessary in the proposed constitution, but would even be dangerous. They would contain various exceptions to powers which are not granted; and on this very account, would afford a colorable pretext to claim more than were granted. For why declare that things shall not be done which there is no power to do?"

Hamilton argued at the time that any powers not directly enumerated to the federal government in the Constitution could not be exercised, so it was unreasonable to require a bill of rights that would specify rights for states and individuals. He even went so far as to say that developing a bill of rights would encourage federal overreach, the explanation being that by enumerating certain powers, the federal government could easily argue that anything not enumerated in the Bill of Rights was not intended to be off-limits to the national government. Given Hamilton's actions during Washington's first administration, it is clear that his objection, while factually correct, was disingenuous; later developments would demonstrate that

---

[9] From *Federalist No. 84*

it was always his intention to overreach Constitutional authority; the Bill of Rights would merely be a hindrance to his lust for federal power. Eventually, the anti-Federalists won the debate, and a total of twelve amendments were drafted and submitted to the states for ratification. Ten of these would be approved by the various state legislatures; they are reprinted here for reference:

> Congress shall make no law respecting an establishment of religion, or prohibiting the free exercise thereof; or abridging the freedom of speech, or of the press; or the right of the people peaceably to assemble, and to petition the Government for a redress of grievances.

> A well regulated Militia, being necessary to the security of a free State, the right of the people to keep and bear Arms, shall not be infringed.

> No Soldier shall, in time of peace be quartered in any house, without the consent of the Owner, nor in time of war, but in a manner to be prescribed by law.

> The right of the people to be secure in their persons, houses, papers, and effects, against unreasonable searches and seizures, shall not be violated, and no Warrants shall issue, but upon probable cause, supported by Oath or affirmation, and particularly describing the place to be searched, and the persons or things to be seized.

> No person shall be held to answer for a capital, or otherwise infamous crime, unless on a presentment or indictment of a Grand Jury, except in cases

arising in the land or naval forces, or in the Militia, when in actual service in time of War or public danger; nor shall any person be subject for the same offense to be twice put in jeopardy of life or limb; nor shall be compelled in any criminal case to be a witness against himself, nor be deprived of life, liberty, or property, without due process of law; nor shall private property be taken for public use, without just compensation.

In all criminal prosecutions, the accused shall enjoy the right to a speedy and public trial, by an impartial jury of the State and district wherein the crime shall have been committed, which district shall have been previously ascertained by law, and to be informed of the nature and cause of the accusation; to be confronted with the witnesses against him; to have compulsory process for obtaining witnesses in his favor, and to have the Assistance of Counsel for his defence.

In Suits at common law, where the value in controversy shall exceed twenty dollars, the right of trial by jury shall be preserved, and no fact tried by a jury, shall be otherwise re-examined in any Court of the United States, than according to the rules of the common law.

Excessive bail shall not be required, nor excessive fines imposed, nor cruel and unusual punishments inflicted.

> The enumeration in the Constitution, of certain rights, shall not be construed to deny or disparage others retained by the people.

> The powers not delegated to the United States by the Constitution, nor prohibited by it to the States, are reserved to the States respectively, or to the people.

The two Amendments that were not passed interestingly had nothing to do with individual rights. The first dealt with the population requirements related to Congressional representation, and the second stipulated that Congressional salary increases, once passed by Congress, could not take effect until after an election had occurred. The first of these amendments was discarded; the second was ratified in 1992 as the 27th Amendment.

It should be noted that the original intent of these amendments was to place limits on federal authority, not to regulate state or local legislation. The practice of incorporation would not become common until the Supreme Court case *Gitlow v. New York* in 1925[10]. Until the mid-twentieth century, it was understood that the bill of rights only applied to the federal government. For example, until incorporation became official policy, it was common for states to have official denominations, and to require good standing membership in a church body as a prerequisite for service in the state legislature. It should also be noted that, while the bill was originally ratified in

---

[10] In *Gitlow v. New York*, Gitlow, a socialist, argued that a New York law which punished certain types of political speech, and under which he was prosecuted, violated the First Amendment. This case, which the Supreme Court decided in Gitlow's favor, marked the start of the general practice of incorporation.

order to limit federal power, the federal government has frequently used it to derive implied powers. For example, the final clause in the fifth amendment was intended to protect private property, but today it is used as an implied power for government to seize private property, as long as the owner is 'justly compensated.' This, of course, shows the irony of Hamilton's statement against the Bill of Rights; his prediction came to pass, even though it is clear in looking back that he made the argument primarily to discourage what he saw as a problematic limitation on federal power.

Today's history classes tend to gloss over the Articles of Confederation, and effectively skip from the end of the Revolutionary War directly to the Constitutional government with only lip service to a weak confederation that did not work. To do this is to modify history and make it seem as though the constitutional government we currently have was a step from monarchy toward liberty; this is not the case. When compared with the Articles of Confederation, it becomes clear that the Constitution was a step from liberty back to monarchy.

As this journey begins, it is fitting to look back to another people who demanded a strong central authority for their common defense. In Old Testament times, Israel was ruled by a council of judges (similar to the Articles' Congress). The people of Israel demanded a king so that they could be ruled. Samuel warned them of the dangers of a king[11]:

> "This is what the king who will reign over you will claim as his rights: He will take your sons and make them serve with his chariots and horses, and they

---

[11] 1 Samuel 8:10-18, from the *New International Version*.

will run in front of his chariots. Some he will assign to be commanders of thousands and commanders of fifties, and others to plow his ground and reap his harvest, and still others to make weapons of war and equipment for his chariots. He will take your daughters to be perfumers and cooks and bakers. He will take the best of your fields and vineyards and olive groves and give them to his attendants. He will take a tenth of your grain and of your vintage and give it to his officials and attendants. Your male and female servants and the best of your cattle and donkeys he will take for his own use. He will take a tenth of your flocks, and you yourselves will become his slaves. When that day comes, you will cry out for relief from the king you have chosen, but the LORD will not answer you in that day."

# Two

# The First Presidency

*"I walk on untrodden ground. There is scarcely any part of my conduct which may not hereafter be drawn into precedent."*
George Washington

The United States Constitution establishes a chief executive in Article II, Section1: "The executive Power shall be vested in a President of the United States of America." Section 1 goes on to describe the requirements for becoming president, and the method of election. In Section 2, the powers delegated to the President are outlined. These powers are as follows:

> The President shall be Commander in Chief of the Army and Navy of the United States, and of the Militia of the several States, when called into the actual Service of the United States;

He shall have Power to grant Reprieves and Pardons for Offences against the United States, except in Cases of Impeachment;

He shall have Power, by and with the Advice and Consent of the Senate, to make Treaties, provided two thirds of the Senators present concur;

He shall nominate, and by and with the Advice and Consent of the Senate, shall appoint Ambassadors, other public Ministers and Consuls, Judges of the supreme Court, and all other Officers of the United States, whose Appointments are not herein otherwise provided for, and which shall be established by Law.

Article II, Section 3 provides for additional presidential responsibilities:

He shall from time to time give to the Congress Information of the State of the Union, and recommend to their Consideration such Measures as he shall judge necessary and expedient;

He may, on extraordinary Occasions, convene both Houses, or either of them, and in Case of Disagreement between them, with Respect to the Time of Adjournment, he may adjourn them to such Time as he shall think proper;

He shall receive Ambassadors and other public Ministers;

He shall take Care that the Laws be faithfully executed;

And shall Commission all the Officers of the United States.

These tasks are all that the President is constitutionally empowered to do in his official capacity. Remember that, in 2011, the executive branch of the federal government employed 2.8 million people, not including military servicemembers or civilian Defense Department employees, and had an operating budget in excess of $1 trillion, not including funds allocated for entitlements, grants, or Department of Defense operations, and you begin to see exactly how far from the Constitution the nation has drifted. To put it more specifically, this trillion-dollar-plus budget is spent by the eleven cabinet-level departments that have been added since the Washington Administration, and which have to specifically enumerated constitutional mandate.

On April 30, 1789, George Washington was inaugurated as the first president of the United States of America. Washington ran for election unopposed, and the only states whose electoral votes he did not win were those of Rhode Island, North Carolina, and New York (The New York legislature deadlocked attempting to choose electors; North Carolina and Rhode Island had yet to ratify the constitution). Washington took the oath of office required by the Constitution: "I do solemnly swear (or affirm) that I will faithfully execute the Office of President of the United States, and will to the best of my Ability, preserve, protect and defend the Constitution of the United States."

In order to fulfill his duties, Washington appointed four executive officials; Secretary of State Thomas Jefferson, Treasury Secretary Alexander Hamilton, Secretary of War Henry Knox, and Attorney General

Edmund Jennings Randolph. These executive offices were established either in order to fulfill specifically enumerated constitutional requirements, or in order to ensure that laws passed by Congress were properly executed. In the cases of State and War, the offices relate directly to Executive powers (the power to command the armed forces and the power to appoint ambassadors and receive foreign dignitaries), while the Treasury department was established by Congress in order to ensure execution of laws passed by Congress related to the coining of money, and to manage government revenue. The Attorney General served as part-time legal counsel to the President, and did not run an executive department (The Department of Justice was not established until 1867).

In addition to these departments, Washington also played a key role in developing the third branch of the new government – the judiciary. In 1789, Congress passed, and Washington signed, the Judicial Act, which gave frame to both the Supreme Court and the lower federal courts. The Act also set the jurisdiction of the federal judicial system; the Supreme Court would have jurisdiction over all disputes between states, between a state and the federal government, any case where a state was a named party, and cases involving diplomats or ambassadors. It was also tasked to rule on any law or action considered to be in violation of the Constitution.

All evidence seems to be that Washington took his constitutional role seriously; this should be no surprise, since he had presided over the convention where the document was developed, and therefore it is not unreasonable to assume that he found the job description suitable. Furthermore, he made an attempt to reconcile with the anti-federalists by appointing Jefferson and Randolph, both outspoken critics of the Constitution, to his cabinet. These gestures, however, would not completely fill the chasm between those supporting a strong federal government and those suspicious of central authority. Before Washington's tenure as President was complete, he would face both a tax revolt, in the form of the Whiskey Rebellion, and a serious division in his cabinet, between Jefferson, the individualist, and Hamilton, the statist. Although history turns a kind eye towards Washington's administration, and there is a general impression that there was harmony and singularity of vision among the founders, a serious study of the first presidency reveals one thing: from the beginning, there have been elements in the United States government intent on centralizing power and overreaching their authority.

### Alexander Hamilton – Architect of an Empire

Alexander Hamilton was so instrumental in the development of the Constitutional government that it has been said that he "more than any other designed the Government of the United States." Hamilton was one of the greatest critics of the Articles of Confederation, considering it to be too weak, and favored an extremely strong central government. During the Constitutional Convention, Hamilton proposed a government structure in which the states would effectively lose all sovereignty and the President and Senators would serve a life term. This proposal had very little chance of success, as it was essentially no different from the British system that the colonists had just fought a war to separate themselves from. In the end, Hamilton was not satisfied with the final version of the Constitution, believing that it was too weak, but he signed it in the knowledge that even in this form, it would be a hard sell to the states. Following ratification, Hamilton exploited the implied powers in order to centralize a number of things that were not enumerated to the federal government in the Constitution, starting a precedent that would slowly erode all state power over the following 220 years. To get a good idea of how Hamilton viewed the United States, the opening paragraph of *Federalist No. 1*, written by Hamilton under the pseudonym Publius, is instructive:

> "AFTER an unequivocal experience of the inefficacy of the subsisting federal government, you are called upon to deliberate on a new Constitution for the United States of America. The subject speaks its own importance; comprehending in its consequences nothing less than the existence of the UNION, the safety and welfare of the parts of which it is composed, the fate of an empire in many respects the most interesting in the world."

The reference to the United States as an empire, though it had only gained its independence seven years earlier, and had no military to speak of, shows the road that Hamilton saw the new country taking. Throughout human history, empires have changed the course of history, but none have been noted for their respect of liberty and individual self-determination. Having just broken free from one empire, Hamilton's desire was to create one of his own, and two of the largest events of Washington's presidency would result from Hamilton's vision.

## The Whiskey Rebellion – The Tea Party, With Liquor

In early America, whiskey was cheap, plentiful, and heavily consumed. There is actually a simple reason for this; in addition to being an excellent social drink, the production of grain liquor is a simple way to convert excess grain into a non-perishable good, which is easy to transport and less likely to spoil than bulk grain. Whiskey was so plentiful in the colonies and territories that it was often joked that you couldn't raise a barn without a barrel. The consumption of whiskey was common throughout the United States, but nowhere more so than along the Appalachian Mountains, which at the time were on the western edge of the country, very distant from the seat of government.

During the Revolutionary War and its immediate aftermath, a large debt, by eighteenth-century standards, had been accumulated. The government under the Articles of Confederation had total debts of $54 million, and the states had combined debts of $25 million. When the Articles of Confederation was organized, all of this debt was consolidated under the national government, since the state debts had in large part been incurred during the struggle for independence. The Articles of Confederation did not grant the federal government the authority to levy taxes; it was assumed that the states would be responsible for their own debts, as well as for funding the operational expenses of the federal government, but the Constitution had granted taxation authority to the Congress. In 1791, under the urging of Treasury Secretary Alexander Hamilton, Congress passed, and Washington signed, a bill levying an excise tax on distilled spirits. This was to be the first tax imposed by the federal government, and would therefore be a test regarding how well the states and their citizens would respond to federal taxation.

That the tax was unpopular is unsurprising. What is surprising, however, was how unpopular it was, particularly along the western border. Westerners in particular claimed two grievances; first, the tax unfairly targeted the west geographically, which was heavily reliant on small-scale distillation operations for its economy, and second, since distillers could either pay a large flat fee or a per gallon fee, the tax provided an unfair advantage to the less-numerous large Eastern distillers, who could pay the flat fee and end up with a much smaller per-gallon expense than the smaller producers.

If both of these complaints sound familiar, they should. When the Declaration of Independence was written 15 years earlier, one of the grievances listed against the king was "For imposing Taxes on us without our Consent." When viewed in historical context, the similarity between the imposition of the whiskey tax on those living in territorial holdings, without Congressional representation, and the taxation of the Colonists who had no representation in London, which led to the Revolutionary War becomes clear.

Prior to the Declaration of Independence, England had fought a long and expensive war against combined French and indigenous Indian forces. The French and Indian War, which lasted from 1754 to 1763, resulted in a huge debt to the British crown. In order to pay this debt, Great Britain began to levy use taxes against a number of goods in the colonies (one of these being tea). Amid cries of "no taxation without representation," the colonists protested these taxes, at one point being so bold as to board a ship full of tea in Boston harbor and dump the goods into the bay. Western Americans similarly felt that a remote federal government was imposing unfair and inequitable taxes against people who were, for the most part, out of sight and out of mind.

As to the complaint that the government developed a tax policy that unfairly benefitted big business at the expense of small business, there is a litany of examples of this throughout the years, but one need look no further than the Patient Protection and Affordable Care Act of 2010. This act, which neither protects patients nor makes health coverage affordable, is so destructive to businesses that over 1500 companies, as of this writing, have been exempted from the law. The catch is that most of these waivers have gone either to mega corporations or to businesses located in districts of members of Congress who supported the act, giving them a government-sanctioned competitive edge against both small businesses and districts that did not support the party in power. Hamilton's whiskey tax benefitted large distilleries along the eastern seaboard, including in his home state of New York, at the expense of their smaller competition out West. Clearly, hypocrisy and government favoritism are not new; they have been with the United States from the first administration.

Washington, who had bills to pay, was faced with a potential insurrection from his citizens. Mobilizing the state militias of New Jersey, Maryland, Virginia, and Pennsylvania, Washington met the rebelling distillers with an overwhelming force of nearly 13,000 men (yet another complaint against the king documented in the Declaration). The rebellion was quickly dispersed, and Washington, true to his words, had established a precedent: unequal taxation may be immoral when it comes from the British crown, but not when it comes from the United States Government. This incident also makes history in that the very first time the President took command of a United States military force, it was against his own people.

Such an analysis of Washington's tax policies may seem unfair; after all, the Constitution had granted the federal government taxation authority, and the government clearly needed a source of revenue in order to cover not only its debt, but ongoing operating expenses. All of these things are true, and it is very clear that, in order for a government to function, a source of revenue is necessary. However, the way that the tax was structured, with those far away from the government forced to bear the burden, and the loophole which granted larger businesses an inequitable advantage, are both too calculated to have been anything other than deliberate. In the event that taxation cannot be avoided, a society dedicated to freedom and equality should have tried harder to make sure that the burden was shared by the population.

### Hamilton's National Bank

Imposition of taxes was not the only priority for Treasury Secretary Hamilton. A strong federalist, Hamilton also proposed the creation of a central bank of the United States, viewing it as an opportunity to strengthen the economy and industry. There really seemed to be only one problem: the Constitution had no provision for establishing banking institutions. This, however, seemed to be of little consequence to Hamilton, who favored appeals to the elasticity of the Constitution's 'implied' powers to get things done. In defense of the bank, Hamilton argued that since the creation of a national bank was not specifically prohibited by the Constitution, it was implicitly allowed. Remember, this is the same exact man, who, in arguing against the Bill of Rights made the statement that "why declare that things shall not be done which there is no power to do?"

Ultimately, in spite of some passionate opposition, both from Congress and Washington's other cabinet members (Jefferson and Randolph opposed the bank, both on principal and constitutional grounds), Hamilton had his way, and the legislation establishing the First Bank of the United States was signed into law by President Washington in 1791.

The bank was chartered to be an independent corporation with initial investment capital of $10 million. Of this, the federal government would purchase shares of $2 million, and the remainder was to be raised through sales of stock to private interests. The only difficulty was that the United States treasury did not technically have $2 million. As was pointed out earlier, the government had accumulated nearly $80 million in debt up to this point. Hamilton's solution was to borrow the $2 million from the bank, then turn around and purchase the required shares using this loan.

### Washington Leaves Office

In 1797, after eight years in office, Washington retired. At this point, he had served in public life for four decades as a statesman, soldier, general, and President. As he predicted at the start of his Presidency, Washington set a number of precedents. By stepping down after a second term, he began a tradition that would be unbroken until FDR (after which the 22nd Amendment made the tradition law). Not all of his precedents were positive, however. Through his support of Hamilton's economic policies, he set the precedent of unequal taxation in favor of big business, of government using force to subdue dissent, of arguing for constitutionally implied powers that effectively give the federal government unlimited authority to do anything not specifically prohibited, and of borrowing money the government does not have for projects and programs that are outside of its mandate. Over the next two centuries, these precedents would be used and built upon, allowing the federal government to become an unstoppable behemoth.

# Three

# Manifest Destiny

*"What a prodigious growth this English race, especially the American branch of it, is having! How soon will it subdue and occupy all the wild parts of this continent and of the islands adjacent. No prophecy, however seemingly extravagant, as to future achievements in this way [is] likely to equal the reality."*
Rutherford B. Hayes

In the Treaty of Paris, which formally ended the Revolutionary War, Britain ceded land not directly tied to the states approximately equal in size to that which made up the original thirteen states, meaning that the United States was actually double the size of the states. Ending at the Mississippi River to the west, the Great Lakes to the north, and the Florida panhandle to the south, this territory became the property of the federal government. For the next twenty years, this land would remain mostly uninhabited; it was only following the war of 1812 that a significant number of people began to push westward. Once this push started, though, it was tough to stop; more and more people began to believe that it was the United States' destiny to stretch from the Atlantic Ocean to the Pacific, and some also believed that the United States would eventually annex Canada (provision for this had even been made as part of the Articles of Confederation). Although the U.S./Canada marriage never took place, a series of events would result in a United States that stretched 'from sea to shining sea.' These events would take several shapes: the Louisiana Territory was purchased, Texas, an independent republic, applied for admission to the Union, the Oregon and Florida territories were ceded by European powers, and most of the Southwest was acquired as the result of a war of conquest fought against Mexico. Throughout all of this expansion, little or no attention was paid to the property claims made by native peoples. As with the development of all empires, a number of these events, when looked at closely, took this nation further from its founding roots, resulting in a larger federal government, more debt, and a less free citizenry.

## The Louisiana Purchase – Jefferson's Federalist Turn

Jefferson was arguably the greatest proponent of individual liberty of the founding generation. During the presidential election of 1800, he wrote in a private letter, "I have sworn upon the altar of God eternal hostility against every form of tyranny over the mind of man." A harsh critic of the Constitution, which he feared would result in a return to monarchy, Jefferson nonetheless accepted George Washington's offer to serve as the first Secretary of State. During his tenure, he feuded bitterly with Treasury Secretary Hamilton over the Constitutional role of the federal government, and what rights it possessed. As covered earlier, Hamilton used the argument that the government had the authority to do anything not prohibited it by the Constitution when arguing for the establishment of a national bank. Jefferson insisted that only things specifically enumerated as part of the federal government's powers could legitimately be done.

In 1800, Jefferson was elected as the third president of the United States. This was a critical period for the fledgling nation; tensions with European powers were high, and settlement into the western territories along the Mississippi River had begun to increase. This increase in settlement quickly brought to prominence the importance of the use of the Mississippi River for the transportation of goods up and down the western border of the United States, and the port city of New Orleans, which allowed river traffic to pass into the Gulf of Mexico and around Florida to the eastern United States. The railroad era would not begin for another thirty years, and effective motorized transportation was still more than a century away, so the most efficient way to move goods from the Western Territory to the larger metropolitan areas along the East Coast was over the water. As a result, in 1803, Jefferson sent James Monroe and Robert Livingston to Paris in an attempt to purchase the city of New Orleans from the French, or at the very least secure a treaty which would allow safe passage along the river and into the Gulf. The offer that would be made by the French, however, was much, much, more: Monroe was told that the United States could purchase the entire Louisiana Territory from France for the sum of $15 million. This would result in a doubling of the United States' size, at a nominal sum.

Jefferson immediately saw the benefit of such a deal; the amount of land being offered would easily contain natural resources worth more than the asking price, and would secure the vital Mississippi River within the boundaries of the United States. For many reasons, it was too good of a deal to pass up.

There was, however, a small problem. The Constitution did not give the federal government the specific authority to make land purchases from other nations. Additionally, the government did not have the money in the treasury to make the purchase; it was eventually made on credit, financed by the British at a rate of 6%. Even though he had concerns regarding the Constitutionality of the purchase, Jefferson determined that the potential benefits justified it, and the United States took official control of the Louisiana territory in a ceremony held in New Orleans on December 20, 1803.

At first glance, the details surrounding this purchase seem very similar to Hamilton's founding of the National Bank in 1791. In both cases, there was a lack of specific Constitutional authority. In both cases, the federal government was required to borrow money in order to make the deal work. In both cases, the President determined that the benefits outweighed the risks, and Congress agreed. There is, however, an important difference: When the United States was founded at the end of the Revolutionary War, the general government possessed a large tract of land, which demonstrates that the founders, even those who were wary of the power of a central authority, were not completely at odds with the idea of the general government owning property, at least until it could be sold off to private interests. Furthermore, while the federal government does lack the Constitutional authority specifically to purchase land, it does explicitly have the power to enter into agreements with other nations, and the purchase of Louisiana was an agreement with France. Perhaps even more important is the fact that

Jefferson clearly wrestled with this issue and the Constitutional problems it may present, while Hamilton was clearly never worried about limitations on federal action.

The larger issue brought up by the Louisiana Purchase though is one of federal versus state power. The original Union was an agreement of states to unite in common defense and welfare. Each state voluntarily joined the union, and considered it a coalition of sovereign entities. With the Constitution, the states agreed (with the exception of Rhode Island, which was more coerced than convinced) to create a federal entity that was their equal, and which assumed certain powers that the states had previously held. To say that the federal and state governments were intended to be equal comes from a clear reading of both the Constitution and the writings of those that supported it. The federal government was to be supreme in matters of foreign relations (war, diplomacy, etc.), while the states were to govern their own internal affairs as they saw fit. However, with the Louisiana Purchase, there was now significantly more land that was not part of a state than land controlled by all of the states put together; all of it effectively under the control solely of the federal government. As these territories grew, and areas applied for statehood, the new states would be entities that had, prior to statehood, been under federal control. Following statehood, these territories would legally become sovereign entities, but the shadow of federal control would never fully recede; these states were a different breed, one that was created by the federal government, not the other way around, and as westward expansion continued, these states would quickly outnumber the original thirteen, from which the federal government was born. It has been said by state's rights advocates that "the states created the federal government, not the other way around," but during the 1800's, this statement would be turned on its head.

## *Florida – America Flexes its Military Muscle*

In 1816, the United States constructed Fort Scott along the border Georgia shared with Florida, which was a territory of Spain at the time. Fort Scott was billed as a way to ensure security along the border, but General Andrew Jackson, who had ordered the construction, had other ideas. The location of the fort made supply by water the best option, but the only waterway, the Apalachicola River, ran through Spanish territory, and past what was known as Negro Fort, home to approximately 300 escaped slaves and a number of Chocktaw Indians. Jackson knew that if he attempted a supply run down the river, his boats would be attacked, and on July 17, 1816 he was proven correct. In retaliation, Jackson immediately ordered the destruction of the fort, which amounted to an act of war against Spain. The Spanish voiced their displeasure, but did little else, as they had neither the power nor the will to defend Florida, which was of limited value. In using an act of deliberate provocation to justify hostilities against others, Jackson would set a trend that would be followed by no fewer than two presidents during the nineteenth century, including the revered Abraham Lincoln.

In 1818, Jackson again crossed the border into Spanish territory while pursuing Seminole Indians. This time, he had been given approval to do so, provided that he did not engage Spanish forces. This instruction went unheeded; Jackson would engage Spanish forces who were helping the Seminoles at St. Marks and Pensacola, and ordered the military executions of two British subjects who were engaged in trade with the Indians and the Spanish.

Spain, which was in negotiations with the United States to sell Florida, backed out of the talks in response to the attacks. Eventually, they realized that they did not have the power to hold Florida, should the United States attempt to take it by force, and ceded the land to the U.S. in exchange for a U.S. agreement to abandon any claims to Spanish lands in modern-day Texas, New Mexico, Arizona, Nevada, Utah, and California. The United States would keep its word; this land would not be taken by force until it belonged to Mexico. For his part in the acquisition of Florida, Jackson would become a folk hero, and was elected as the seventh president of the United States in 1828. While land had been taken from native peoples by force for most of the United States' history, this marked the first time since its founding that land was acquired by threat of force against a 'civilized' European world power.

The problems with this acquisition, both moral and Constitutional, should be clear. If Jefferson was worried about the Constitutional implications of purchasing land, how much greater are the implications of taking it by threat of force? Jackson not only defied direct orders from superiors, but committed an act of war against a foreign power without a declaration of war from Congress, a Constitutional requirement. Congress seemed to understand the implications of this behavior at the time; a formal resolution condemning Jackson's actions was prepared, but never passed due to his popularity among the public. Instead, his election to the Presidency ten years later shows that the American public has long been willing to overlook virtually any violation of the rule of law for a leader whom they like.

### *The Republic of Texas*

As part of the acquisition of Florida from Spain, the United States agreed not to pursue claims on the Texas territory, which included most of modern-day Texas, along with parts of New Mexico, Oklahoma, and Colorado. In 1836, Texas became an independent republic, declaring its independence from Mexico in a document based heavily on the United States' declaration. Like its predecessor, the Texas declaration contained a list of Mexico's violations of the natural rights of Texas' citizens, and formed the legal framework for separation. For nine years, Texas would operate as an independent nation, but agreed to annexation and applied for American statehood in 1845. As the 28th state, Texas shares a critical common trait with the original thirteen colonies; it had for a time operated as an independent republic, as the original thirteen had done under the Articles of Confederation. Through the entire period of Manifest Destiny, from 1800 until the Civil War, the acquisition of this territory most closely resembles the admission to the Union envisioned by the original founders, without the use of force or purchase of property by the federal government.

## *Mexican Cession of 1848*

While the entry of Texas into the Union may be relatively free of Constitutional complications, it quickly led to an action which more closely resembles the acquisition of Florida. This time, however, the activity would be undertaken under the direct orders of a sitting United States president, and is yet another step toward complete federal control and empire.

As noted previously, proponents of Manifest Destiny saw the borders of the United States stretching from the Atlantic to the Pacific. To the west of Texas, the land from the Texas border to the Pacific was controlled by

Mexico, a nation that was far weaker militarily than the United States. In 1845, President James K. Polk sent a diplomatic envoy to Mexico in an attempt to purchase this property; his offer was rebuffed, as Mexico had never accepted Texas' independence and was upset at the U.S. for annexing the republic.

In the absence of a diplomatic solution, Polk decided on a military one. Troops under the command of General Zachary Taylor had been ordered to the Rio Grande River, an area under disputed ownership between Mexico and Texas. American troops even briefly crossed the river and blocked the Mexican port of Matamoros. In retaliation to what was rightly seen as a violation of its sovereignty, Mexican troops attacked Taylor's men, killing eleven of them. Polk immediately requested a declaration of war against Mexico from Congress, which he received in May, 1846.

Given the fact that Polk had entered office with a mandate to secure the Republic of Texas and the lands to the west, and his clear attempt to provoke a conflict with Mexico after his offer of land purchase was denied by the Mexican government, these words from Polk's third annual address to Congress seem particularly disingenuous[12]:

> "It has ever been our cherished policy to cultivate peace and good will with all nations, and this policy has been steadily pursued by me. No change has taken place in our relations with Mexico since the adjournment of the last Congress. The war in which

---

[12] As with much of the material in this work, this address is available in numerous locations. In this case, it was retrieved from the American Presidency Project.

the United States were forced to engage with the Government of that country still continues.

I deem it unnecessary, after the full exposition of them contained in my message of the 11th of May, 1846, and in my annual message at the commencement of the session of Congress in December last, to reiterate the serious causes of complaint which we had against Mexico before she commenced hostilities.

It is sufficient on the present occasion to say that the wanton violation of the rights of person and property of our citizens committed by Mexico, her repeated acts of bad faith through a long series of years, and her disregard of solemn treaties stipulating for indemnity to our injured citizens not only constituted ample cause of war on our part, but were of such an aggravated character as would have justified us before the whole world in resorting to this extreme remedy. With an anxious desire to avoid a rupture between the two countries, we forbore for years to assert our clear rights by force, and continued to seek redress for the wrongs we had suffered by amicable negotiation in the hope that Mexico might yield to pacific counsels and the demands of justice. In this hope we were disappointed. Our minister of peace sent to Mexico was insultingly rejected. The Mexican Government refused even to hear the terms of adjustment which he was authorized to propose, and finally, under wholly unjustifiable pretexts, involved the two countries in war by invading the territory of the State of Texas, striking the first blow, and shedding the blood of our citizens on our own soil.

Though the United States were the aggrieved nation, Mexico commenced the war, and we were compelled in self-defense to repel the invader and to vindicate the national honor and interests by prosecuting it with vigor until we could obtain a just and honorable peace. On learning that hostilities had been commenced by Mexico I promptly communicated that fact, accompanied with a succinct statement of our other causes of complaint against Mexico, to Congress, and that body, by the act of the 13th of May, 1846, declared that "by the act of the Republic of Mexico a state of war exists between that Government and the United States." This act declaring "the war to exist by the act of the Republic of Mexico," and making provision for its prosecution "to a speedy and successful termination," was passed with great unanimity by Congress, there being but two negative votes in the Senate and but fourteen in the House of Representatives.

The existence of the war having thus been declared by Congress, it became my duty under the Constitution and the laws to conduct and prosecute it. This duty has been performed, and though at every stage of its progress I have manifested a willingness to terminate it by a just peace, Mexico has refused to accede to any terms which could be accepted by the United States consistently with the national honor and interest."

In the end, Polk had his way: for a total of $15 million, paid as a war settlement, the United States acquired all of the lands north of the Rio Grande and west of Texas, including modern-day California, Arizona, Nevada, Utah, and the remainder of New Mexico.

During the war, an agreement was made settling the ownership of the Oregon Territory between the United States and Great Britain. Therefore, only one small section of the contiguous United States remained; the Gadsden Purchase, which extended modern-day Arizona and New Mexico to the south, was made by President Franklin Pierce in 1853. This land was seen as needed for the completion of the transcontinental railroad. The huge purchase price, however, at $10 million, is seen by many as an admission of the wrongs related to the Mexican-American War and an attempt to compensate for the provocation of war.

### *The Department of the Interior – "The Department of Everything Else"*

By 1849, the land holdings of the federal government far exceeded those of the states, and it was determined by Congress that a new federal bureaucracy was needed to manage all of the new property. Therefore, in 1849, Congress established the Department of the Interior, the first Cabinet-level department to be established since Washington's first Cabinet was assembled. Duties and operating units of several of the other departments were shifted to the Department of the Interior, including the Bureau of Indian Affairs, the General Land Office, and the Patent Office.

With the establishment of this Department, a dangerous precedent was set in motion. While several of the Department's original tasks had Constitutional foundations, such as managing Indian Affairs and providing patents, these few Constitutional activities were hardly enough for a Cabinet-level bureaucracy. Additionally, the federal government had spent the last 50 years obtaining land by any means necessary, including baiting a neighboring country into war, and now had a need to manage that land. As a result, the Department of the Interior grew into a number of roles that had no Constitutional mandate. One example of this is the administration of federal lands. In 1812, the General Land Office was established with the purpose of selling federally-owned lands acquired both through the Revolutionary War and the Louisiana Purchase. Although the only federal land specified in the Constitution was the ten square miles provided for the federal capital, the federal government would never fully divest itself of its other property, and following the expansions in the first half of the nineteenth century, the vast amount of land now under federal control required management, which would fall under Interior's jurisdiction, and would become consolidated under the Bureau of Land Management in 1946.

In addition to land management, the Interior Department operates a number of other agencies, including the Bureau of Reclamation, the United States Fish and Wildlife Service, the United States Geological Survey, the Bureau of Ocean Energy Management, Regulation, and Enforcement, the National Park Service, and the Office of Surface Mining. Detailing the Constitutional overreach of each of these agencies is beyond the scope of this work, but one example, involving the Bureau of Reclamation, proves instructive, and serves as an example of other overreaches of federal authority.

The Bureau of Reclamation's stated mission "is to manage, develop, and protect water and related resources in an environmentally and economically sound manner in the interest of the American public." This mission sounds all well and good, until the Constitutional implications are considered. The Constitution provides no authority to the federal government for the management of water or related resources; the only way that the government could argue that it possessed this authority would be to argue that it had primary authority over federally-owned lands (of which the Constitution did not grant authority to own). The lie to this argument would be revealed the following century, when, according the Bureau itself, "Because Texas had no Federal lands, it did not become a Reclamation state until 1906 when Congress passed a special Act including it in the provisions of the Reclamation Act." This would become a regular feature as the nation grew; if the federal government did not have Constitutional jurisdiction over a particular area, it would take over anyway, and few states would have the courage to challenge a government that had accomplished a complete takeover of the New World in such a short order.

At the close of the first decade of the 21st century, the Department of the Interior employed close to 75,000 people, and had a 2010 operating budget of $20 billion. For such a massive expansion of federal authority and oversight, it would seem necessary for the Constitution, which details the structure and delegation of authority of the government, to be modified. However, the only amendment to the Constitution passed during the Manifest Destiny period of 1800-1853, was the 12th (1804), which revised procedures related to Presidential election. This means that during the first half of the nineteenth century, the executive branch expanded dramatically, but with no accompanying expansion to federal authority documented in the Constitution, implying either that the authority for federal land management had always been there, or that the pretense of using the Constitution to determine the size and scope of the executive branch had been abandoned already.

The 50 years from the Louisiana Purchase to the Gadsden Purchase were a busy time. The nation, having adopted the Constitution just over a decade before Jefferson took office, would expand from its border on the Mississippi River all the way to the Pacific, and encompass all of what are considered the contiguous 48 states today. This expansion would result in a formidable empire, but like all empires, the growth came at a dramatic cost. Twice, the United States would provoke foreign nations into war, and attempt to claim the moral high ground because they were fired upon. In every expansion, with the possible exception of Texas, the federal government would acquire more land, which it would eventually grant to states, reversing the founding ideal that it was the states that created the federal government, not the other way around. Finally, a fourth Cabinet-level department would be founded, and over the years expand well beyond any semblance of Constitutionally-based authority. The period of Manifest Destiny plays a pivotal role in United States history; the period where the seat of power transitioned from state control to the central government. This shift of power would set the stage for the next key period in United States history – the Civil War.

# Four

# The Civil War

*"I think it better to do right, even if we suffer in so doing, than to incur the reproach of our consciences and posterity."*
Robert E. Lee

It is quite likely that there is no period in United States history more misunderstood than the founding. The reasons for secession from Britain, and the political philosophy that motivated our struggle for independence are often misrepresented or warped through the lens of modern understanding and the political motivations of the educating class. If, however, there were to be a close runner-up, the Civil War would be it, and frequently for the same reasons.

To even begin to defend the southern secession of 1861 immediately places the defender at a disadvantage; the prevailing modern interpretation is that the South was full of racist, backwoods hillbillies and oppressive plantation owners. Even more difficult is the fact that this is, to some degree, true. It is important, though, to understand that racism was rampant across the whole of the United States, not just in the South, and slavery was practiced in states on both sides of the war. It is also important to recognize that to our modern sensibilities, the predominantly agrarian South feeds into our own prejudices against rural life as uneducated and intellectually simple. A thorough study of the Civil War, and the philosophical issues surrounding it, reveal a much more complicated situation, and one in which the critical question – who is in charge, the states or the federal government – would be answered at the cost of 625,000 lives and the sovereign liberty of millions in posterity.

### *Slavery: The Abominable Institution*

No analysis of the American Civil War can be deemed complete without a discussion of the institution of slavery. While there are numerous issues related to the War Between the States, if you were to ask ten American high school students to list the primary driver behind the Civil War, at least six would respond 'slavery' (and at least two would give you a blank stare, but the federalization and subsequent collapse of the education system is a topic for another chapter). Therefore, any work that attempts to legitimize the secession of the southern states must first address this issue if it wishes to be taken seriously.

From the beginning, the slave distribution was uneven among the colonies. The northern colonies had been established by persecuted religious groups, while southern colonies were established with the goal of exploiting the New World's natural resources. As the colonies grew into trade centers, the North focused primarily on manufacturing and shipping, while the South continued to focus on resource exploitation through large commercial agricultural operations. These operations required a huge labor source, and African slave suppliers and European slave traders were more than willing to provide a seemingly endless labor pool from across the Atlantic.

Slavery was a contentious issue even during the Constitutional Convention. As highlighted earlier, many of the founders held a view of natural law that emphasized the equality of man and the immorality of one man controlling another. This view is at complete odds with the institution of slavery, and the fact that many of those same founders were slave owners is a hypocrisy that was not lost on the men themselves, though they dealt with the cognitive dissonance in different ways. Thomas Jefferson, an ardent supporter of abolition through the mid-1780s, gradually quieted his public objections to what he had once referred to as an "abominable crime." In his later life, Jefferson would adopt a view that considered blacks so inferior in intellectual ability that slavery was actually a beneficial institution. Given that he also believed that the division between North and South over slavery would eventually erupt into war, it is not clear if he actually believed his justifications, or was merely trying to make peace in order to preserve the nation that he had helped create. Benjamin Franklin, who had owned slaves in his early years, took a different approach. Becoming convinced that slavery was a moral evil, he became a staunch abolitionist, arguing for the abolition of slavery to be included in the Constitution and petitioning Congress for abolition after it was not. George Washington and George Mason, both Virginians like Jefferson, were slave owners who publicly recognized that slavery was at odds with founding principles. Both desired to see both the slave trade and the spread of slavery in the United States stopped, but seemed at a loss as to how to emancipate those already in bondage.

On the brink of the Civil War, not much had changed. Many public figures in the United States, both in the North and the South, recognized that slavery was a moral evil, but those in the South, like the founders before them, seemed unable to determine how to transition an economy so heavily reliant on slavery to one without it. Of course not all public figures were convinced of the evils of slavery; several prominent Northerners were slave owners, men such as Ulysses S. Grant and William Sherman, who would become two of the North's most celebrated generals. Ulysses S. Grant had no intention of fighting a war to end slavery, or even of giving up his rights to own slaves. With regard to the Civil War, Grant allegedly stated to a reporter from the Chicago Tribune[13] that "The sole object of this war is to restore the Union. Should I be convinced it has any other object, or that the government designs using its soldiers to execute the wishes of the abolitionists, I pledge to you my honor as a man and a soldier I would resign my commission and carry my sword to the other side." General Sherman had similar feelings: "I am honest in my belief that it is not fair to my men to count negros as equals. Let us capture negros, of course, and use them to the best advantage."

If there was some level of agreement amongst the political class (men like Grant and Sherman notwithstanding) regarding the immorality of slavery, there was far more consensus that, while Blacks should not be enslaved, they were clearly inferior to Whites. Compare these two quotes:

---

[13] This quote is disputed, and was never published by the Tribune. The fact of Grant's slave ownership, however, is not disputed.

"I will say then that I am not, nor ever have been in favor of bringing about in anyway the social and political equality of the white and black races – that I am not nor ever have been in favor of making voters or jurors of negroes, nor of qualifying them to hold office, nor to intermarry with white people; and I will say in addition to this that there is a physical difference between the white and black races which I believe will forever forbid the two races living together on terms of social and political equality. And inasmuch as they cannot so live, while they do remain together there must be the position of superior and inferior, and I as much as any other man am in favor of having the superior position assigned to the white race. I say upon this occasion I do not perceive that because the white man is to have the superior position the negro should be denied everything.[14]"

"The condition of slavery with us is, in a word, Mr. President, nothing but the form of civil government instituted for a class of people not fit to govern themselves. It is exactly what in every State exists in some form or other. It is just that kind of control which is extended in every northern State over its convicts, its lunatics, its minors, its apprentices. It is but a form of civil government for those who by their nature are not fit to govern themselves. We recognize the fact of the inferiority stamped upon that race of men by the Creator, and from the cradle to the grave, our Government, as a civil institution, marks that inferiority.[15]"

---

[14] During his fourth debate with Stephen Douglas in September, 1858

The second quote, which compares black slaves to convicts and lunatics, is from Jefferson Davis, the first and only president of the Confederate States of America. The first, which states that blacks are incapable of living with whites in social and political equality, is from the "Great Emancipator" Abraham Lincoln. Given that the two men shared such similar feelings regarding black slaves, it becomes less difficult to believe that the Civil War was not actually about slavery.

American slavery, like the Civil War as a whole, is not a simple topic, and to frame it as a North vs. South issue is to do it a disservice. While slavery was recognized as a moral evil by many in the United States, even by slave owners themselves, it would still be practiced both by the Union and the Confederacy through the entire war. It is also clear that even those who may have recognized the evils of slavery believed blacks to be deeply inferior to whites, and were not predisposed to fight a war on their behalf. However, the first seven southern states to secede would list slavery as the primary cause for their separation from the Union. Perhaps the best way to classify the role of slavery in the Civil War is to recognize it as a primary factor in several of the southern states' decision to secede, but also to realize that the Union fought the war for its own reasons, and slavery was not among them.

### Tensions Rise Between North and South

As previously noted, North and South had developed very different economies by the mid-nineteenth century. The northern states had developed a highly

---

[15] During a speech in the Senate chambers in February, 1860.

industrialized economy, focused on manufacturing and urban development, while states in the South had remained more rural, focusing on agriculture and centering their communities on large, privately-held plantations rather than on urban centers, and in this economy, cotton was king. In fact, the booming British textile industry imported 75% of its raw cotton from the United States' southern region, and the income from these exports greatly increased the United States' ability to obtain foreign credit. Immediately prior to the Civil War, the southern states accounted for 70% of all United States exports, much of this being cotton.

There was a problem, however. While the South was growing rich exporting raw materials, the northern industrial sector was becoming stagnant. Britain, a competing industrial center, had the ability to produce goods much more cheaply, and prices for British goods, even in the southern United States, were less than the same goods produced in the New England states. As a result, the South was sending a large percentage of its raw materials across the Atlantic, and then purchasing manufactured goods back from Britain, effectively cutting out the northern states.

The North, with the larger white population and, therefore, more political power, responded by enacting a series of protective tariffs in Congress during the first half of the nineteenth century. These tariffs were designed to raise the cost of British goods to the levels of Northern goods and therefore increase Northern sales in the Southern states. These tariffs hit a high point in 1828, when the so-called "Tariff of Abominations" levied a 62% tax on nearly all imports. This tariff had a twofold devastating effect on the Southern economy: goods cost significantly more than they had previously, and when

Southerners began to import less from Britain due to the high taxation, the British, faced with a reduced market for their textiles, responded by purchasing less Southern cotton. The end result was a South that took a dramatic hit in terms of income, and rightfully blamed the protectionist tariffs supported by the North for this situation. Over the next twenty years, tariffs would be lowered in 1832/33, raised again in 1842, lowered yet again in 1846, and lowered in 1857. Following the start of the Civil War, tariffs would again be raised in 1861. This rollercoaster of tariff rates would have effectively the same result as permanently high rates. Since Southerners would never know from one year to the next what the tariff rates would be, they would be forced to buy manufactured goods from the North as a hedge against potential tariff increases.

Although the tariffs imposed on imported goods were a source of much animosity between the North and the South, the issue of slavery, or specifically the issue of escaped slaves, caused an even bigger divide between the two regions. As mentioned earlier, while slavery was not at issue in the prosecution of the Civil War, it was the primary reason cited by the original seven states that seceded. These states, South Carolina, Georgia, Florida, Alabama, Mississippi, Louisiana, and Texas, specifically refer in their secession declarations to the refusal of northern states to return escaped slaves – a direct requirement of Article IV, section 2 of the Constitution, which states:

> "No Person held to Service or Labour in one State, under the Laws thereof, escaping into another, shall, in Consequence of any Law or Regulation therein, be discharged from such Service or Labour, but shall be delivered up on Claim of the Party to whom such Service or Labour may be due."

Although abolitionists clearly hold the moral high ground in this situation, the fact remains that to harbor an escaped slave or hinder those hunting for escaped slaves was a violation of the Constitution. While the total number of slaves who escaped was miniscule in comparison to the number of slaves in the South (census figures put the number of escaped slaves at around 6,000 while the slave population in the U.S. was around 4 million), the psychological impact was significant.

Slavery and Manifest Destiny were also closely intertwined. As the nation expanded into the West, and new territories applied for statehood, Southerners became increasingly worried that the admission of new states with anti-slavery majorities would end up tilting the balance of power in Washington, D.C. to the point where slavery could be outlawed nationally. This tension would result in several compromises between the North and South that would temporarily alleviate some of the tension, but never completely, and never for long.

The first of the compromises, the Missouri Compromise, occurred in 1820, and was actually intended to allay the fears of northerners who feared the expansion of slavery into new states. Since the issue of slavery had not been addressed in the Constitution, it was left for the states to decide if slavery would be legal within their borders. In the North, where industrialization and maritime activities had replaced much of the agrarian economy, slavery was not seen as an economic necessity, and as a result, the morally repugnant nature of the institution had gained more widespread acknowledgement, with the outcome that many (though certainly not all) of the states in the northern half of the nation had outlawed the practice. In 1820, Missouri requested admission to the Union as a slave state; at the time, the balance of states where slavery was legal to states where slavery was illegal was even at fourteen, and the admission of Missouri as a slave state would have tipped the balance in favor of slavery. As a compromise, Maine was also admitted to the Union as a free state, keeping the balance. Furthermore, as a result of the compromise, it was determined that all states admitted to the Union from the Louisiana Territory north of 36°30' would be admitted as free states. This compromise, although intended to keep everyone happy, actually had the unintended effect of cementing the divide between the North and South. As Thomas Jefferson wrote regarding the compromise[16]:

> "A geographical line, coinciding with a marked principle, moral and political, once conceived and held up to the angry passions of men, will never be obliterated; and every new irritation will mark it deeper and deeper. "

In this prediction, Jefferson demonstrates his typically astute understanding of human behavior. Although slavery was practiced in several of the states north of 36°30', this line would effectively demarcate the region that eventually seceded from the Union. From the time of the Missouri Compromise until the War broke out, this line divided the North and South.

In late 1860, tensions between North and South had reached a boiling point. The North had managed to severely cripple the South's economic success through the imposition of protectionist tariffs, and was routinely ignoring Constitutional requirements to return escaped slaves. At this point, very little provocation was required for the South to act. This small provocation would come in

---

[16] In an 1820 letter to John Holmes. Transcript available through the Library of Congress at http://www.loc.gov/exhibits/jefferson/159.html

the form of the presidential election of 1860 and the election of Abraham Lincoln. While Lincoln himself was far from being an abolitionist, he was a member of the newly-formed Republican Party, which had strong abolitionist support. Sensing that their grievances would receive little in the way of support from the new administration, seven of the southern slave-holding states made the decision to dissolve their ties to the Union.

### *Secession*

It is important to understand that secession was not a controversial idea in the mid-nineteenth century. At the time that the Constitution was ratified, the states viewed themselves as sovereign, and considered the Union to be a sort of joint venture among the states to further common defense and foreign policy objectives. As members in such a venture, the states assumed that they had the right to dissolve their ties with the other states, and the Union itself, for proper cause, or even no cause at all. Virginia, along with several other states, specifically reserved the right to secession in their ratification documents. According to Virginia's ratification[17]:

> "WE the Delegates of the people of Virginia... DO in the name and in behalf of the people of Virginia, declare and make known that the powers granted under the Constitution, being derived from the people of the United States may be resumed by them whensoever the same shall be perverted to their injury or oppression..."

---

[17] As with the minutes from the ratification convention, this passage was taken from the U.S. Constitution online.

This clause makes clear that the people of Virginia, and the state in which they resided, intended to maintain their own sovereignty, and maintained their right to remove themselves from the Union should they determine that the Union had exceeded its authority and in so doing injured the citizens of the state.

It is also important to highlight that the southern secession of 1860-1861 was not the first time that a region had contemplated secession from the Union. During the administrations of Thomas Jefferson and James Madison, a number of trade embargoes with Great Britain were enacted due to increasing tensions with the foreign power; tensions which would erupt in war in 1812.

Both the embargoes and the war had a devastating impact on the New England states, as the economy in this region revolved primarily on shipping, the majority of which was done between the United States and Great Britain. In reaction, delegates from the states of Massachusetts, New Hampshire, Vermont, Connecticut, and Rhode Island met in secret in Hartford, Connecticut from December 15, 1814 to January 5, 1815 to discuss solutions to their crisis. One of the solutions proposed was secession, and although this solution was never put into action, it is a clear indication that secession was commonly understood to be a right of the Union's member states.

In this historical context, the decision by South Carolina to secede in December 1860 seems far more reasonable. The legislature of South Carolina, like the delegates to the 1776 convention 84 years earlier, believed that it had been irrevocably wronged by the federal government, and that redress from grievances was not forthcoming. In their "Declaration of the Immediate Causes Which Induce and Justify the Secession of South Carolina from the Federal Union," South Carolina refers to the Declaration of Independence, stating that "whenever any form of government becomes destructive of the ends for which it was established, it is the right of the people to alter or abolish it, and to institute a new government." South Carolina did this in the final, legally binding paragraph of the Declaration[18]:

> "We, therefore, the People of South Carolina, by our delegates in Convention assembled, appealing to the Supreme Judge of the world for the rectitude of our intentions, have solemnly declared that the Union heretofore existing between this State and the other States of North America, is dissolved, and that the State of South Carolina has resumed her position among the nations of the world, as a separate and independent State; with full power to levy war, conclude peace, contract alliances, establish commerce, and to do all other acts and things which independent States may of right do."

The secession of South Carolina prompted action on the part of six other states: Georgia, Florida, Alabama, and Mississippi all voted to secede from the Union in January of 1861, and Texas followed on February 2, 1861. The secession declarations from the other six states closely resemble South Carolina's by referring to the right granted in the Declaration of Independence for citizens to abolish and change their government in the event that the existing government no longer serves them.

---

[18] A copy of the South Carolina secession document can be viewed at the Yale Law School's Avalon Project:
http://avalon.law.yale.edu/19th_century/csa_scarsec.asp

To the seven states which broke ties with the Union, this was the end of the issue. Representatives were recalled from Congress, and the states went about their regular business. The seven seceding states re-formed in February 1861 under a new constitution as the Confederate States of America. The Constitution of the Confederacy, interestingly, is a near-identical copy of the United States Constitution; some sections are even word-for-word copies. The structure included the three branches of executive, legislative, and judicial, and each maintained the same responsibilities it had held under the Union constitution. The Confederate constitution protected the right to slavery in Article I, Section 9, but outlawed importation of slaves from any nation other than the United States in the same section. The similarities in the constitutions of the Union and the Confederacy demonstrate that it was not a disagreement with respect to the fundamental structure of government that motivated the secession, but what the South viewed as a movement away from the Constitution.

While the North's response to the secession and formation of the Confederacy is unsurprising, it is at the very least hypocritical. Had the federal government practiced intellectual consistency, and continued to operate on the same principles under which it was founded, there would have been no Civil War, and the United States of America and the Confederate States of America would quite possibly be living side-by-side to this day. In the Declaration of Independence, Jefferson had written that "it is the Right of the People to alter or to abolish [government], and to institute new Government, laying its foundation on such principles and organizing its powers in such form, as to them shall seem most likely to effect their Safety and Happiness." In their secession documents, all seven of the states that seceded in late 1860 and early 1861 had relied on this statement, and provided the reasons for secession in their documents. In doing nearly the same thing that the original thirteen colonies had done a century earlier, the South effectively put to the test the principles that had been enshrined in the Declaration of Independence. And in the North's response, it demonstrated that the central authority in Washington D.C. had effectively taken King George's place.

It is also likely that, given diplomatic pressure from the United States and Great Britain, along with internal opinion, the CSA would have abolished slavery on its own. This situation, over a century and a half later, would likely have been better for the liberty of all Americans, since the existence of two Americas would have put in place economic market pressures that do not exist today, due to a homogeneous, unified America. Alas, this situation was not to be; the United States had no intention of allowing the southern states to pull out of an agreement which they had entered into freely, and it was the typical incentives of money and power, not the abolition of slavery, which would motivate the forced preservation of the Union.

### *Fort Sumter – A Remake of an Old Classic*

Following the War of 1812, a series of coastal fortifications were constructed along the eastern seaboard to protect vital shipping ports. In 1827, construction began on just such a fortification in Charleston Harbor. This fortification, named Fort Sumter, after Revolutionary War hero Thomas Sumter, was not yet complete when South Carolina seceded from the Union in 1860. Following the notification of secession, federal troops had abandoned inland forts in South Carolina, deeming them indefensible in the event that the South Carolina militia was to decide to take them by force. One hundred and twenty-seven men from E and H companies, 1ˢᵗ U.S. Artillery, led by U.S. Army Major Robert Anderson, secretly relocated to the unfinished fort in Charleston Harbor.

Once discovered by the South Carolina government, the new occupants of Ft. Sumter were asked on numerous occasions to leave; all requests were declined or simply ignored. South Carolina rightly considered this rock outcrop their property, and to have soldiers loyal to what now amounted to a foreign power occupying this space was not acceptable.

The Union was now left with two options: either abandon the fort, effectively recognizing South Carolina's independence, or attempt to hold the fort, which would require resupplying it. An attempt to resupply would likely be seen by South Carolina as an act of aggression; in fact, an initial resupply attempt in January 1861 had been repelled by gunfire from South Carolina military cadets. It is important for the events that follow to note that the occupants of Fort Sumter were not under siege; they had been asked to leave, and there is no indication that they would have been hindered in any way from returning to United States soil should they have complied. Therefore, no resupply of the Fort was necessary for the preservation of life, and the only likely outcome of such an attempt would be war.

In order to set the events which would follow in proper perspective, it is necessary to understand what losing the South meant for the United States. As mentioned previously, the South was the major export center for the nation; a full 70% of all U.S. exports came from the states which had seceded. Furthermore, the South was a huge source of income for the North, because following the implementation of import tariffs, the South either purchased an increased amount of goods manufactured in the North, or paid exorbitant tariffs to Washington in order to purchase British goods. Either way, the North benefitted greatly from Southern agriculture. While the history books record great speeches and essays about the noble goal of preserving the Union, the motivation for maintaining that bond was money and power, not the lofty notion of brotherhood and unity so often presented. In his book *A Century of War: Lincoln, Wilson & Roosevelt*, John Denson highlights the financial benefit that the North received from the South:

> "Another development which began to divide the North and South was that the political power of the North allowed it to keep a vast majority of the tariff revenue and use it for "internal improvements," such as building harbors and canals, which was, in effect, a corporate welfare program."

In fact, President Lincoln's inaugural address, delivered on March 4, 1861, gives a hint as to what was to come. In addressing the secession of the southern states, Lincoln, who had already publicly stated that he believed the secession illegal, declared that[19]:

> "The power confided in me will be used to hold, occupy, and possess the property and places belonging to the government, and to collect the duties and imposts; but beyond what may be necessary for these objects, there will be no invasion, no using of force against or among the people anywhere."

---

[19] Also available at the Avalon Project:
http://avalon.law.yale.edu/19th_century/lincoln1.asp

The keys to this statement can be found in the declaration that government property would be held, and that duties and imposts would be collected. The fact is, the United States would be in serious financial trouble without the "duties and imposts," and it would be through the holding of government property that the solution would be found.

If the Union could not afford financially to lose the South, neither could it be seen as the aggressor in the conflict. To openly declare war against the seceding states would undoubtedly be seen as the action of an empire attempting to keep hold of its property, not unlike the actions of Great Britain following the declaration of the United States' independence. Knowing this, Lincoln had publicly declared that force would not be used in order to bring the South back into the Union's fold. Fortunately, a method for making the South appear the aggressor, and the North simply attempting to right an errant child, was available at Fort Sumter. Like President Polk in Mexico, and General Andrew Jackson before him in Florida, President Lincoln would commit an act designed specifically to bait his opponent into striking first: the resupply of Fort Sumter would take place.

To claim that Lincoln deliberately planned the resupply of Fort Sumter to provoke a war with the Confederacy is a serious accusation, but it is not without historical support. In his diary entry for July 3, 1861, Illinois senator Orville Browning recounts a topic of conversation with President Lincoln during a meeting on that day:

> "[Lincoln] himself conceived the idea, and proposed sending supplies, without an attempt to reinforce, giving notice of the fact to Governor

Pickens of S.C. The plan succeeded. They attacked Sumter — it fell, and thus, did more service than it otherwise could."

This entry demonstrates that to his political confidantes, Lincoln had spelled out the plan that was to initiate the Civil war, leaving the North blameless, and the South the aggressor. Lincoln was correct, the resupply attempt at Fort Sumter had the desired effect. The South Carolina militia, under the command of Colonel James Chestnut, Jr., opened fire on the fort at 4:30am on April 12, 1861, approximately five hours after the first resupply ship from the Union arrived at the fort. Although Union soldiers were eventually forced to abandon the fort, the overall mission had been successful; the Union now had the excuse it needed to take back the Confederate states by force. It should be noted that not all of the remaining states in the Union fell for this ruse; the states of North Carolina, Virginia, Tennessee, and Arkansas, understanding that the Union was the aggressor in the battle, and would attempt to permanently solidify its control over the states, seceded following the battle at Fort Sumter.

### The War and Its Aftermath

The actual fighting of the war itself, while of historical importance, is outside the purpose of this work. Far more critical to the causes of liberty and freedom are the precursors and the aftermath. Two points, however, from midway through the war, are of key importance: the Emancipation Proclamation and the Gettysburg Address.

On January 1, 1863, Abraham Lincoln issued the Emancipation Proclamation, an executive order freeing all slaves in states still under Confederate control. This executive order is interesting for several reasons, and results in a case study of the growing expansion of federal power and confusion of separated powers within the federal government.

Early in the war, some Union generals had taken the position that slaves in Confederate territory were war contraband, and therefore the Fugitive Slave Act, which required state and federal officials to return escaped slaves to their owners, regardless of the legality of slavery in the state of capture, was void. Additionally, these generals tended to free the slaves in Confederate territory that they managed to capture. This presented a very real legal problem for the Union. It was the Union's official position that the southern states were in rebellion, and that the secession was legally irrelevant; therefore, slaves in captured area could not be declared contraband of war, since the Union was not fighting a war with another nation, but attempting to quell an internal rebellion. Lincoln's message to his generals was clear: slaves were not war contraband and could not be freed. Generals who refused to comply were replaced. However, Congress reversed this decision, passing legislation in March 1862 which made it illegal for Union generals to return fugitive slaves.

In June 1962, Congress passed legislation that outlawed slavery in U.S. territories, which seems an appropriate Congressional action, as the lands in question were Federal property and not within the boundaries of any state (one wonders how the issue would have been handled had the institution of slavery survived, and some of these territories become states. Would the states have been allowed to settle the slavery issue for themselves? Or would they have been required to abide by the territorial law? This, of course, leads only to speculation, and not historical analysis. It does, however, serve to highlight the problem with the federal government owning large tracts of land highlighted in the last chapter, as well as the greater problem that the founders failed to properly deal with slavery, as Franklin implored them to do). Congress continued the drive against slavery in territorial holdings and states in rebellion; in July 1862, it passed the "Second Confiscation Act," which freed slaves held by anyone in rebellion against the Union. Lincoln, however, objected to this legislation, arguing that as Commander in Chief, he held sole authority over the rebel territory, and only he could free those slaves when and if he determined that it was a proper military measure. With the Emancipation Proclamation, issued six months later, Lincoln took the same action that Congress had attempted earlier. The Proclamation curiously exempted the city of New Orleans, which was under Union control, as well as 13 surrounding Louisiana parishes. It is unclear why Lincoln chose to leave approximately 300,000 individuals in area controlled by his troops, and in his opinion subject to his sole authority as Commander in Chief, enslaved.

With the argument between Congress and Lincoln over control of the rebel states, the history of the Emancipation Proclamation showcases the amount of power that Lincoln possessed during the conflict, and helps to demonstrate yet again that all that is needed for the president to act as a king is military conflict. Like FDR would do 80 years later with the internment of Japanese citizens, Lincoln was able to seize complete power within the borders of the United States by provoking a military conflict and then declaring all area within the conflict his to control. The Emancipation Proclamation also exposes a great irony; once slaves were freed in Confederate territory, the only place in the United States where slavery was practiced was in the Union. In fact, the states of Kentucky and Delaware continued to allow slavery after the end of the War, and were only stopped when the thirteenth amendment went into effect in December 1865.

The Gettysburg Address is a far less convoluted subject, but also demonstrates the disingenuous nature of politicians. The entire address, at 278 words, is one of the shortest, but most famous, presidential addresses in all of American history. What makes it so important to our understanding of freedom; however, is its dishonesty. The final lines of the speech, which are familiar to school students across America, are as follows[20]:

> "It is rather for us to be here dedicated to the great task remaining before us -- that from these honored dead we take increased devotion to that cause for which they gave the last full measure of devotion -- that we here highly resolve that these dead shall not have died in vain -- that this nation, under God, shall have a new birth of freedom -- and that government of the people, by the people, for the people, shall not perish from the earth."

In this speech, Lincoln takes for the Union the mantle of freedom and self-directed government. This, of course, is directly contrary to the actual situation. The people of the Confederate States of America, upon due consideration, had decided that life under the governance of the United States of America no longer served their purposes. Their elected representatives in the state legislatures, in accordance with this sentiment, cut ties with the Union and, in the same spirit as in the Declaration of Independence, "institute[d a] new Government, laying its foundation on such principles and organizing its powers in such form, as to them shall seem most likely to effect their

---

[20] From the Avalon Project:
http://avalon.law.yale.edu/19th_century/gettyb.asp

Safety and Happiness." In the aftermath of the Civil War, there would be freedom for those released from the bondages of slavery, but there would also be a death of freedom; the idea that a group of individuals would have the right to cut ties with a government that they felt no longer served them, and reorganize as they saw fit, would die along with the Confederacy.

Following the conclusion of the war, the former Confederate states were placed in a state of martial law while new state governments could be established. This period, known as Reconstruction, would be a period in which freedom was completely suppressed, and the goals of black equality and state reorganization would fail miserably, and likely led to greater resentment of newly free blacks than would have been the case if no reconstruction had been attempted. During reconstruction, all governmental decisions were dictated from Washington, and any person who had held a position of authority in the Confederacy was barred from holding public office. This was certainly not a situation where "government of the people, by the people, for the people" was practiced, and it cemented the idea, begun during the Westward Expansion, that it was the federal government, not the states, which were in charge.

During reconstruction, the equality of former slaves would be enforced by federal overseers; this greatly angered many southern whites, and enabled those motivated by racism to convince their fellow citizens that black freedom was closely intertwined with federal tyranny. Therefore, with forced reconstruction, the seeds of racial tension which persist in the South to this day were cemented in the southern psyche.

### Outcomes of the Civil War and Reconstruction

If there was any positive outcome of the Civil War, it was the abolition of slavery. Although it did not play a part in the North's decision to force the South to remain in the Union, it became clear during the course of the war that no Union could exist divided over this issue. While this is a positive outcome, it was an inevitable outcome regardless of whether the South remained in the Union. The Confederate States of America would have had the United States and Great Britain as its chief trading partners. Great Britain had already abolished slavery prior to 1861, and with an abolitionist majority in the United States, abolition would have followed quickly. Sentiment against slavery in Great Britain was already beginning to strain trade relations with the South by the time the CSA was formed, and with similar economic pressure from the United States, abolition in the CSA was all but a foregone conclusion.

In addition to external pressures, there were contemporary economic philosophers that believed internal economic pressures would have eventually led to the collapse of the institution of slavery. In 1863, Irish economist and author John Elliott Carnes published *The Slave Power: Its Character, Career, and Probable Designs*[21] , which was an attempt to understand and explain the reasons for the death of slavery in the North and its healthy survival in the South. According to Carnes, it was clear that the death of slavery in the North had nothing to do with moral objections to the institution; instead it became economically infeasible. Carnes saw a near future in which

---

[21] A free copy of this work is available through Google Books, at: http://books.google.com/books?id=OmgZG_bQT80C&printsec=frontc over&source=gbs_ge_summary_r&cad=0#v=onepage&q&f=false

the South would face the same economic reality. While many educated Whites of the time saw Africans as fundamentally inferior, Carnes believed the opposite, and claimed that, if freed, black slaves would become considerably more effective laborers:

> "There is not a tittle of evidence to show that the aversion of the negro to labour is naturally stronger than that of any other branch of the human family. So long as he is compelled to work for the exclusive benefit of a master, he will be inclined to evade his task by every means in his power, as the white man would do under similar circumstances; but emancipate him, and subject him to the same motives which act upon the free white labourer, and there is no reason to believe he will not be led to exert himself with equal energy."

Once slave owners understood that they could pay free blacks and receive more efficient labor than by compelled work, the institution of slavery would be doomed; after all, it would take a racist of a particularly evil and foolish disposition to not take advantage of the most economically viable and efficient source of labor. Therefore, to credit the Civil War with an end to slavery is perhaps premature; the most likely situation is that it merely shortened it by a few years, and at a terrible cost.

Indeed, if anything, the Civil War and Reconstruction created a situation in the South where race relations were irrevocably poisoned. Had the CSA abolished slavery on its own, the animosity toward free blacks would very likely not have taken root the way it did in the aftermath of the war. After all, if a man comes to a conclusion about something based upon his own reason, he is far more likely to accept it and move on than if he is forced to accept another man's conclusion under threat of force. This is a universal truth, not one particular to Reconstruction. Equality enforced at the end of the Union's gun in the form of martial law created a deep animosity in white southerners towards both the North and freed slaves. This animosity would manifest itself in Black Codes, Jim Crow laws, and a policy of segregation that would continue as official policy for a century, and still persists unofficially in some regions to this day.

The actual ramifications of the Civil War are actually far more insidious when viewed through the lens of personal liberty. In 1776, in declaring their independence from Great Britain, the founders had declared that it was appropriate for men to govern themselves, and that they could, according to the Laws of God and Nature, modify or abolish their governments should they believe that it could be done better. In 1777 and again in 1787, the original thirteen states had voluntarily entered into a compact with one another for mutual benefit. However, during the period of westward expansion in the early nineteenth century, the federal government began to take a more prominent role, as it acquired property through purchase and conquest. As new states formed from this property, the federal government was more and more seen as the source of the states, instead of the other way around, as it had been at the founding.

With the Civil War, this transition was complete. States, including those which had been around at the beginning, were told at the point of a gun that they did not have the right to break ties with the Union, and that the central authority was supreme. The fears of the Anti-Federalists had come to fruition; the central government had become the master, and state sovereignty was dead. With this question settled, the federal government was now free to expand virtually unfettered – the Progressive Era was set to begin.

# Five

# Progressivism Takes Root

*"Of all tyrannies a tyranny sincerely exercised for the
good of its victims may be the most oppressive."*
C.S. Lewis


Following the Civil War, the United States changed
both quickly and dramatically. Rail power had come into
its own during the war, and transcontinental rail lines
allowed the rapid and inexpensive transportation of both
goods and people from one coast to another. The ease in
transport allowed manufacturers to consolidate operations
in fewer locations, and gigantic regional factories began to
replace the smaller production operations that had
traditionally dotted the landscape. With this consolidation,
more and more Americans found themselves working for a
corporation instead of themselves, and living in urban
areas instead of small towns and rural expanses.

In addition to advances in rail transportation, three new technologies would be developed in the late nineteenth and early twentieth century that would revolutionize the way people worked and lived. First, during the 1870's, a number of developments in the field of electrical engineering would result in the first power plants, light bulbs, and commercially-distributed electricity in the world. In the 1880's, Nikola Tesla would perfect the alternating-current system, which allowed for convenient electricity generation and transmission across long distances. The availability of electricity would make industrial production easier than ever thought possible. Second, in 1885, the first modern automobile would be produced in Germany by Karl Benz. Although an historic development in its own right, the automobile would also lead to the development of the assembly line by Henry Ford in 1908. This development led quickly to high-speed mass production of nearly every common consumer good, making these goods cheaper and more readily available than at any time in history. Today, the Henry Ford Museum in Dearborn, Michigan, is a testament to Ford's impact on manufacturing; nearly half of the floor space is dedicated not to automobiles, but to the home and farm technology that were produced using the assembly line.

In the midst of this upheaval in the way Americans conducted their day-to-day lives, a new class of politicians would arrive on the scene. This new breed of political leader, who would come to be known as a Progressive, would argue that the fundamental changes in American life warranted fundamental changes in American political structure. Progressives sold these changes as efforts to protect worker's rights, improve working conditions, eliminate child labor, ensure clean food and drinking water, and give the average American more control over the political process. According to Progressive icon Woodrow Wilson, in his book *The New Freedom*:

> "The life of the nation has grown infinitely varied. It does not centre now upon questions of governmental structure or of the distribution of governmental powers. It centers upon questions of the very structure and operation of society itself, of which government is only the instrument. Our development has run so fast and so far along the lines sketched in the earlier day of constitutional definition, has so crossed and interlaced those lines, has piled upon them such novel structures of trust and combination, has elaborated within them a life so manifold, so full of forces which transcend the boundaries of the country itself and fill the eyes of the world, that a new nation seems to have been created which the old formulas do not fit or afford a vital interpretation of."

In his writings, Wilson claimed that the Constitution was outdated, and that the nation had reached a point where it was not recognizable from the one that was organized under the Constitution in 1789. As a result, he argued, the old rules no longer applied, and new ones must be implemented. As demonstrated with his actions as President, Wilson proved true to his words.

The claims that the new social landscape requires a new type of politics, and promises a new type of freedom, are simply false. Many of the actions taken by Progressives were attempts to limit personal liberty and freedom in an effort to produce a more 'acceptable' society, including Prohibition, the only Constitutional amendment which directly limited personal and commercial freedom. In reality, Progressives would manage to use many of these issues to foment class warfare, conduct social engineering experiments, create a regulatory environment that to this day cripples production and innovation, and subject the average American to the tyranny of mob rule. This era would also begin the American policy of foreign military interventionism, resulting in a military-industrial complex that now consumes 46% of the world's military budget. Additionally, if Manifest Destiny resulted in the transfer of primary authority from state authority to central authority, and if the Civil War ended the idea of state sovereignty for good, then the Progressive Era would not only serve to further empower the central government, but continue a shift of power within that government from the Legislative Branch to the Executive.

### *America – From Representative Republic to Direct Democracy*

In order to fully appreciate the political shift which would take place in the first part of the twentieth century, it is important to go all the way back to the Constitutional Convention of 1787. In the development of the Constitution, the United States was formed as a representative republic instead of a direct democracy, and for a specific reason. The founders, who at least in principle feared an all-powerful monarch (although the final version of the Constitution would set up the potential for just that), also had a healthy fear of the ignorance of the average citizen, who they believed would generally vote in his own immediate interest without considering the big picture. Additionally, many of the founders, inspired by the political philosophy of John Locke, believed in divinely-ordained rights that should not be subject to popular whim. With his usual wit, Benjamin Franklin described the problem thusly: "Democracy is two wolves and a lamb voting on what to have for lunch. Liberty is a well-armed lamb contesting the vote." In this quote, we see the problems that would result from an unrestrained pure democracy – the people will vote in their own best interest, even when it harms others in the minority. He also shows the necessity of protection against unrestrained democracy, because if the lamb has the unalienable right to bear arms, it prevents the wolves from enacting the results of the vote.

There were a number of ways that the founders attempted to prevent the mob rule inherent in a pure democracy. First, the central government was structured with three separate branches, each with the ability to check the other's powers. Second, the only individuals directly elected to the central government by citizens were members of the House of Representatives. The members of the Senate were chosen by the state legislatures, and the President was chosen by electors, who were also chosen by the state legislatures initially; this practice was changed to election by popular votes by all states during the first half of the nineteenth century. The reasons for these practices were twofold; first, it was assumed that state legislators would be more well-informed than the public at large. Second, this method was a way to maintain state sovereignty.

In addition to these electoral procedures, rights considered inviolable were enumerated in the Bill of Rights. A direct democracy has no such document, because in a direct democracy, it is the will of the majority, not the God-given rights of individuals, which are of primary concern. In *Federalist No. 10*, James Madison recognizes this problem:

"From this view of the subject it may be concluded that a pure democracy, by which I mean a society consisting of a small number of citizens, who assemble and administer the government in person, can admit of no cure for the mischiefs of faction. A common passion or interest will, in almost every case, be felt by a majority of the whole; a communication and concert result from the form of government itself; and there is nothing to check the inducements to sacrifice the weaker party or an obnoxious individual. Hence it is that such democracies have ever been spectacles of turbulence and contention; have ever been found incompatible with personal security or the rights of property; and have in general been as short in their lives as they have been violent in their deaths. Theoretic politicians, who have patronized this species of government, have erroneously supposed that by reducing mankind to a perfect equality in their political rights, they would, at the same time, be perfectly equalized and assimilated in their possessions, their opinions, and their passions."

In 1787, it was understood that direct democracy was a threat to individual liberty. However, during the Progressive Era, the American people were promised a more direct democracy under the guise that it would lead to more control over their government. In reality, what was being attempted was the final nail in the coffin of state control over federal authority. This would occur in 1913, when the passage of the seventeenth amendment changed the appointment of Senators from the choice of the state legislatures to direct popular election. With electors for the presidency already being chosen by popular vote, this meant that state legislatures had lost all control over the central government.

The reasons for an attempt to establish more direct democracy are exactly related to the arguments against direct democracy highlighted in Federalist No. 10. Progressive politicians were already working to establish defined factions amongst the electorate, first by appealing to income class, and later to sex, race, and cultural differences. By creating a more direct democracy, politicians could then manipulate these factions into voting a particular way and by creating majorities made up of different factions, these factions could be used for Progressive purposes, but no single faction would ever have enough power of its own. In the Progressive Era, the best example of this factional divide can be seen in the imposition of the income tax, which was officially authorized by the sixteenth amendment to the Constitution in 1913. Progressives, led by President Woodrow Wilson, were able to manipulate class divisions such that a majority of voters supported a progressive income tax, where higher wage earners had to pay an ever-larger percentage of their income to the federal government. The wealthy, representing a very small percentage of the electorate, had no chance to fight such an initiative. Although this would not be the last time the tyranny of the majority would be exercised, it is certainly one of the most pervasive in American history, and demonstrates that, in a direct democracy, the two wolves are certainly capable of voting themselves a rack of lamb for lunch.

## *A New Corporate Regulatory Environment Emerges*

During the latter part of the nineteenth century, a new type of business was born: the mega-corporation. These mega-corporations are exemplified chiefly by the Standard Oil Company, founded by John D. Rockefeller, and U.S. Steel, which was helmed by J.P. Morgan. These corporations grew into massive entities by merging with and acquiring their competitors until nearly none was left; at its peak, Standard Oil controlled 90 percent of the kerosene business in the United States, while U.S. Steel commanded 67 percent of the American steel market when it was founded in 1901; this share would eventually peak at 80 percent.

When Teddy Roosevelt became president in 1901 following the assassination of William McKinley, the public was very suspicious, and in some cases openly hostile, toward these massive corporations. America's first antitrust law, the Sherman Act, had been passed in 1890, although it had not been strongly enforced. Roosevelt, however, made it a top priority of his administration to aggressively go after corporations that were deemed to be monopolizing industries.

It is at this point that commonly understood and oft-repeated history separates significantly from reality. It is the commonly-received wisdom that corporations such as U.S. Steel and Standard Oil used shady business practices in order to undercut and buy out their competition, so that they could monopolize their markets and force the public to buy their goods at whatever price they asked. Furthermore, it is implied that these predatory practices are an indictment of unrestrained capitalism, and that the federal government was forced to step in to protect the American people. These commonly-held 'truths,' upon further inspection, turn out to be far from the actual truth.

Before continuing, it is instructive to take a moment to properly understand the terms 'free market' and 'capitalism,' since both are regularly misused by those who wish to consolidate power. First, to be a free market supporter does not mean to be pro-big business; instead it is the belief that the private sector should operate without government oversight and without government support. In a true free market system, there is no business that is "too big to fail," government does not use the corporate tax code either to encourage certain behaviors nor to promote the purchase of domestic goods over imported goods via protectionist tariffs, and there are no subsidies or regulations in place to promote or require the production or consumption of a particular good or service. In a free market system, it is the individual that determines what they wish to buy or use, and therefore the individual ultimately determines the success or failure of a private enterprise. Austrian economist Ludwig von Mises, who was studying economics in Europe at the time of America's Progressive Era, argued that free markets and man's freedom were inseparable[22]:

> "This, then, is freedom in the external life of man, that he is independent of the arbitrary power of his fellows. Such freedom is no natural right. It did not exist under primitive conditions. It arose in the process of social development and its final completion is the work of mature Capitalism."

Therefore, for the purposes of this work, free markets are understood to be markets where there is no governmental interference outside of the classical liberal understanding that government exists to protect life and

---

[22] From *Socialism: An Economic and Sociological Analysis.* Free copy available through Google Books.

personal property, and capitalism is understood to mean that the means of production are privately owned and directed towards profit. With these definitions in mind, it is fairly simple to demonstrate that the abuses which led to the mega-corporations are not the result of a free market system, and that the reforms proposed by Progressives are simply an example of government using more government to solve a problem that was created by too much government.

The real historical facts are that the United States government has been regulating markets and colluding with big business for nearly the entirety of its existence. As discussed previously, the very first tax levied by the United States government in 1791 was designed to, at least in part, give large distilleries a competitive advantage over smaller ones. In addition to internal taxes, protectionist tariffs designed to promote the purchase of Northeastern-produced goods were a major factor in the secession of the southern states prior to the Civil War. In his 1776 book *The Wealth of Nations,* considered to be the founding document of liberal free market thinking, Adam Smith cautions against collusion between big business and government:

> "To widen the market and to narrow the competition, is always the interest of the dealers...The proposal of any new law or regulation of commerce which comes from this order, ought always to be listened to with great precaution, and ought never to be adopted till after having been long and carefully examined, not only with the most scrupulous, but with the most suspicious attention. It comes from an order of men, whose interest is never exactly the same with that of the public, who have generally an interest to deceive and even

oppress the public, and who accordingly have, upon many occasions, both deceived and oppressed it."

Alexander Hamilton, the chief architect behind George Washington's economic policy, and therefore the man who set the economic tone for the fledgling nation's economic future, was a vocal opponent of Smith's. In his 1791 *Report on the Subject of Manufacturers*[23], Hamilton specifically argues for both government support of business and the narrowing of competition through the use of tax policy, specifically that of protective tariffs:

> "When former occupations ceased to yield a profit adequate to the subsistence of their followers, or when there was an absolute deficiency of employment in them, owing to the superabundance of hands, changes would ensue; but these changes would be likely to be more tardy than might consist with the interest either of individuals or of the Society. In many cases they would not happen, while a bare support could be ensured by an adherence to ancient courses; though a resort to a more profitable employment might be practicable. To produce the desireable changes, as early as may be expedient, may therefore require the incitement and patronage of government.
>
> The apprehension of failing in new attempts is perhaps a more serious impediment. There are dispositions apt to be attracted by the mere novelty of an undertaking -- but these are not always those

---

[23] Available as a PDF from the National Humanities Center at: http://nationalhumanitiescenter.org/pds/livingrev/politics/text2/hamilton.pdf

best calculated to give it success. To this, it is of importance that the confidence of cautious sagacious capitalists both citizens and foreigners, should be excited. And to inspire this description of persons with confidence, it is essential, that they should be made to see in any project, which is new, and for that reason alone, if, for no other, precarious, the prospect of such a degree of countenance and support from government, as may be capable of overcoming the obstacles, inseperable from first experiments.

The superiority antecedently enjoyed by nations, who have preoccupied and perfected a branch of industry, consitutes a more formidable obstacle, than either of those, which have been mentioned, to the introduction of the same branch into a country, in which it did not before exist. To maintain between the recent establishments of one country and the long matured establishments of another country, a competition upon equal terms, both as to quality and price, is in most cases impracticable. The disparity in the one, or in the other, or in both, must necessarily be so considerable as to forbid a successful rivalship, without the extraordinary aid and protection of government."

From the opinions of the nation's first Treasury Secretary, it is clear to see that far from being a lack of government oversight that led to mega-corporations, it was pro-American big business government policies that allowed these mega-corporations to flourish, and that this was not an unintended consequence of government policy, it was the purpose. In truth, from 1789 through the Civil War, every policy coming from Washington D.C. was specifically designed to promote the industrial economy of the North; the fact that such practices, combined with shady dealings on the part of the corporations (conveniently overlooked by politicians) worked is what led to this point, not unrestrained free-market capitalism.

The Progressive Era would continue the practice of supporting big business on one hand, while at the same time enacting a new slate of regulations designed to 'protect' the public from these businesses. The end result of these concurrent practices would be that the big companies remained big, but with government oversight, and small companies, facing the same regulation, would be unable to compete. To Progressives like Roosevelt, this represented the ideal situation. Roosevelt believed that monopolies were good for the American public, because they were efficient and able to provide goods at low prices due to a lack of competition and the economy of scale that comes with being a large corporation. All that they needed was government oversight to make sure that they did not take advantage of their commanding market share. In his first annual Congressional address, he stated that the government should "assume power of supervision and regulation over all corporations doing an interstate business."

True to his word, during Roosevelt's tenure as president, the government would take on an increasing role regulating business. In 1903, the Department of Commerce and Labor was established as a Cabinet-level department, the first new cabinet department since the Department of Agriculture was established (this department achieved Cabinet-level status at the beginning of the Progressive Era, in 1889). As its name suggests, the Department of Commerce and Labor was intended to develop and enforce regulations related to business matters. According to the legislation establishing the department, its primary purpose was to "foster, promote and develop the welfare of working people, to improve their working conditions, and to advance their opportunities for profitable employment." The Department of Labor's historical archives describe the founding of the department as "the direct product of a half-century campaign by organized labor for a 'Voice in the Cabinet.'" Both of these statements should give pause, as the stated purpose of the Department does not contain a Constitutional mandate, and the creation of a Cabinet-level department to further the cause of a special interest group, in this case organized labor, gave that special interest group a disproportionate level of influence and access. That level of authority and access has only grown; in 1913, the Department of Commerce and Labor would be split into two Cabinet-level departments: the Department of Commerce and the Department of Labor. While neither of these departments has a strictly Constitutional mandate, they currently account for nearly $114 billion of the annual federal budget, and employ 61,000 bureaucrats. The Department of Commerce, ostensibly acting within its constitutional bounds to 'regulate interstate commerce' has routinely stepped in to regulate private industry to a level never intended by the founders of the United States. For example, In 1905, at Roosevelt's urging, Congress passed the Hepburn Act, which authorized the Interstate Commerce Commission to set price caps for rail fares. This marked the first time that the federal government asserted its non-existent authority to determine what prices a private corporation could charge for its services.

In much the same way, the Department of Labor has routinely disregarded constitutional roles; in this case in order to further the cause of organized labor. The pressure exerted by organized labor on the Department of

Labor has become increasingly obvious; in 2011, at the urging of union lobbyists, the National Labor Relations Board, part of the Department of Labor, killed a plan by Boeing to build its new 787 Dreamliner aircraft at a facility in South Carolina, insisting that it had to be built by union labor in Seattle, Washington. Such naked preference for organized labor at the expense of a private corporation's interests shows just how much influence special interest groups have managed to exert over the federal government, and also how far the federal government has overstepped its bounds.

Throughout the administrations of both Presidents Taft and Wilson, the expansion of regulation would continue. In 1912, the Radio Act was passed, which required radio stations to be licensed by the government. This was originally intended to limit interference with military radio frequencies, but would lead to the creation of the Federal Communication Commission, a federal agency which regulates the words that can and cannot be uttered on television, has at several times attempted to implement the so-called Fairness Doctrine, which would force broadcasters to give equal time to opposing political viewpoints (in direct violation of the First Amendment), and most recently has endeavored to regulate internet access through 'net neutrality' regulations. This serves as just one more example of a federal agency established with a mandate that is tenuously constitutional at best, only to expand well beyond that mandate into a monster with no ties to original federal authority and that believes it can limit rights specifically denied the federal government in the Bill of Rights.

In addition to increased market regulations, the federal government would begin regulating the conditions of workers inside of corporations. These regulations would be primarily focused on worker safety, and were a response to hazardous conditions, particularly those found in the steel industry. Amidst these regulations were the first mandatory Worker's Compensation requirements, which required businesses to maintain insurance coverage for workplace injuries. Ironically, these regulations were largely met with favor by big business, which could afford the insurance premiums, and knew that they would place a disproportionate burden on the finances of their smaller competitors. They were met with criticism by organized labor, which saw such an insurance program as a limitation on workers' rights to sue in court over negligent working conditions. In fact, rather than being a step toward worker safety, the worker's compensation apparatus can be seen as yet another early tool of corporatism; a regulatory scheme that benefits big business at the expense of small business and labor. It should also be noted that in some cases, organized labor is clearly the beneficiary of government actions, while in other cases; the benefit is just as clearly given to big business. Rather than being contradictory, this serves as a large-scale example of the sectionalism that the Progressive Era gave birth to and nurtured. Both big business and organized labor are beneficiaries of government largesse, but only through continual patronage, and both can either be blessed by government attention or turned against one another by government-created crises, as those in power see fit. Furthermore, it should also be noted that through it all, the small business and individual American are always disenfranchised.

Despite all of the regulation during this period that benefitted both big business and organized labor at the expense of small business and independent workers, the most ominous development for the cause of liberty would not be legislation, but a new practice which completely replaced legislation: the practice of administrative rulemaking.

Prior to the Progressive Era, legislation dealt with specific issues, and, while not always strictly in keeping with the spirit and intent of the Constitution, at least the proper branch of government was making the law. However, during the first two decades of the twentieth century, legislators decided that the topics they were legislating were becoming too technical, and the volume of legislation required too large. However, instead of recognizing that perhaps the problem was that too much of the market was being legislated, and that perhaps the federal government was overstepping its bounds in legislating things that members of Congress had no expertise in, the solution arrived at was to develop and pass broad legislative framework authorizing an executive department, such as the Department of Labor, to create specific regulations, provided that they could be tied to the overall purpose of the framework. This shift resulted in the movement of rule-making power from the legislative branch, which has the Constitutional mandate for rule-making, to the executive branch, which constitutionally is responsible for rule enforcement. It also moved rule-making away from those directly answerable to voters and into an unelected bureaucracy. Interestingly, this practice had the effect of re-insulating the rule-makers from the public at large, so what Progressives had managed to do was sell the American public the Seventeenth Amendment as a way to have more control over their government, only to turn around and sequester much of the government's power in massive regulatory bureaucracies that had absolutely no accountability to the average American. This practice, where government decision making was moved from the legislature, where the Constitution placed it, to sectors which had no need to worry about election or accountability, would also be applied to United States monetary policy in the form of the Federal Reserve, which would take Congress' authority to coin money, and would not be directly accountable to any branch of government.

## *The Federal Reserve System*

In October of 1907, an attempt was made to corner the market on the stock of the United Copper Company. In order to understand a market corner, it is first necessary to understand the concept of a short sale. Short sellers borrow stock in a company, which they then sell at current market prices. If the price of the stock then drops as a result of the increase in shares available on the market, the short seller buys shares at the lower price to repay the borrowed shares. The difference between the price the borrowed stock was sold at and the price that the replacement stock was purchased at becomes a profit for the short seller. An attempt to corner stock occurs when an individual purchases large quantities of stock in a company in order to reduce availability of the stock. Short sellers who have borrowed stock in the company are then forced to buy shares for repayment from the individual who has cornered the market, usually at a price far higher than they sold the borrowed stock for. In the case of United Copper, Otto Heinze borrowed a small fortune from banks in New York City in order to purchase stock in United Copper in an attempt to corner the market. Heinze, however, underestimated the amount of publicly available stock, and when he forced those who had borrowed stock to repay the shares, they were easily able to obtain shares on the market from sources other than Heinze, and at lower prices. Heinze was left with a massive amount of stock valued at less than the amount he had borrowed to purchase it. As word of this failed attempt to corner the market got out, there was a panic among depositors at the banks Heinze had borrowed from, with a large number of depositors attempting to empty their accounts.

For those not familiar with the banking system, it is common practice for banks to only hold a small fraction of the total value of deposits on hand. This practice, known as fractional banking, allows bankers to make loans using depositor money. This system generally works, as there are few occasions when depositors attempt to withdraw en masse. However, when this does occur, the bank can be left without the funds to oblige the depositor's request, which is exactly what happened in 1907. This panic spread to banks not even involved with the United Copper affair, and by the time the panic subsided in November 1907, consumer confidence in the banking industry had been severely shaken.

This being the Progressive Era, the preferred solution was to grant additional control over the economy to the government. The result of this would be the creation of the third incarnation of a United States central bank; this one with the authority to regulate both the money supply and the entire banking industry. While this may seem like a blow to the big Wall Street banks that were blamed for the 1907 panic, this is far from the case. The truth of the matter, like the regulations on industry, is far more complicated, and reveals yet more collusion between government and big business. From the late nineteenth century, Wall Street bankers had been agitating for a new central bank, because like their cousins in the steel, railroad, and oil industries, they saw government regulation as a way to keep smaller banks from being competitive, and desired a bank with the power to regulate the elasticity of currency to keep them from having to tighten their belts when depositors withdrew large amounts. Simply put, the creation of a central bank with regulatory authority would benefit large Wall Street banks by creating a government-sanctioned banking cartel and by ensuring that members of that cartel were always flush with cash.

In 1913, Wall Street and progressive politicians got their wish. A third central bank was created. Called the Federal Reserve Bank, this bank would serve as the federal government's official bank, and would have the authority to coin and print currency on the government's behalf. The Fed, as it came to be known, had ultimate authority to determine the amount of legal U.S. currency available at any given time, and was set up as an independent entity with minimal oversight and the ability to implement monetary policy without the approval of any official in either the Executive or Legislative branch.

The creation and persistence of the Fed has been sold to the public as protection against the kind of banking panic that occurred in 1907. However, the reason that these panics can now easily be averted is that in the event of a cash shortage, the Fed has the authority to print up as much cash as is needed at any given time. The real loser here is the American public, which has been subjected to steady inflation since 1913: for every dollar spent in 1913, $22.80 has to be spent on the same goods in 2011. Since legal tender currency prior to 1913 was tied to a tangible standard, the American public was protected against the kind of inflation that results from an arbitrary expansion of the money supply, meaning that inflation from 1789 to 1913 was at or near zero. Economist and historian Murray Rothbard sums up the Federal Reserve by comparing it to similar government/big business cartels: "The railroads and shippers had the ICC [Interstate Commerce Commission], the farmers had the Agriculture

Department, and the bankers had the Federal Reserve Board."

### *Prohibition: The [Ig]Noble Experiment*

Progressivism spanned many topics, from the way that government was structured to the areas that they claimed control over, but the entire progressive enterprise was based on a single notion – that the solution to society's ills was government intervention and regulation. This notion did not spring into existence overnight, however; the first 120 years of the nation's history was a slow move toward a more centralized authority, just as the anti-federalists had warned. Despite the growing power and control Washington exerted over the states and their residents, however, few laws had yet been enacted which directly limited individual liberty. This would change in 1919 with the Eighteenth Amendment, which outlawed the manufacture, transportation, and sale of alcoholic beverages. Later legislation would define alcoholic beverages as any beverage which contained more than 0.5% alcohol and exempted alcohol consumption as part of religious practices or medical treatments.

Beginning in the mid-nineteenth century, groups such as the Women's Christian Temperance Movement and the American Temperance Society joined forces with a number of Protestant denominations such as the Methodists, Baptists, Presbyterians, Disciples of Christ, Congregationalists, Quakers, and Scandinavian Lutherans to promote the idea of an alcohol-free United States. These groups had differing reasons for promoting temperance; the religious groups condemned the consumption of alcohol as a sin, while the women's groups contended that as a practical matter, alcohol was damaging to the family. In either case, however, the goal was not to convince individuals that alcohol should be avoided; they intended to use the power of the state to compel compliance with their moral conviction.

Temperance movements had been successful in a number of states, as well as at the local level; Maine had the first statewide prohibition law, which was in effect from 1851-1856; by the time national prohibition went into effect in 1919, over half of the states would have a prohibition law in effect; several of these laws, including Kansas, North Dakota, Mississippi, Oklahoma, and North Carolina would remain in effect following the repeal of national prohibition in 1933. To this date, a number of counties, particularly in the south and mid-south regions, prohibit the sale of alcohol. In fact, Lynchburg, Tennessee, the home of the world-famous Jack Daniel's whiskey distillery, is seated in a dry county, meaning that while Jack Daniel's whiskey is produced in Lynchburg, it cannot legally be sold for consumption within the county boundaries.

In 1916, prohibition had gained national attention, and the elections of that year were expected to be a referendum on the issue. Prohibitionists in both major parties won big; when the new Congress convened in 1917, supporters of prohibition outnumbered opponents by more than 2-to-1. When the United States entered into World War I in April 1917 by declaring war on Germany, the prohibitionists had the perfect excuse to enact nation-wide prohibition: the considerable amount of grain consumed in the distillation of liquor would be put to much better use feeding the troops fighting in Europe. This argument was a smoke screen, and not a legitimate argument; the prohibitionists had supported outlawing alcohol prior to the outbreak of the war, and certainly before U.S. involvement, and wine, which does not require the use of grain, was outlawed alongside beer and grain liquor, which do. Nevertheless, the prohibitionists had their way, and the eighteenth amendment was officially ratified on January 16, 1919, and implemented with the Volstead Act on October 28, 1919. The Act allowed a grace period until January 17, 1920, at which point the manufacture, transportation, or sale of any beverage containing more than 0.5% alcohol would be a federal crime. In order to enforce this law, some 1500 federal agents were hired. Ironically, World War I, the issue that had provided a patriotic cover for prohibition, ended in 1918, two years before prohibition went into effect.

By any objective measurement, prohibition was a miserable failure. The grace period of the Volstead Act was used by many to stockpile wine and liquor for personal consumption. Since the Act did not specifically prohibit alcohol consumption, just the manufacture, transport, or sale, those who purchased massive quantities prior to implementation were legally permitted to imbibe in the comfort of their own homes. Additionally, the exemptions for religious and medicinal purposes prompted dedicated drinkers to either find God or a permissive physician who would prescribe alcohol the way modern physicians in California prescribe marijuana for those suffering from any number of ailments. And for those who could not stockpile, or find a suitable religion or malady, liquor flowed freely at the hundreds of thousands of illegal bars around the country. These establishments, which were known as 'speakeasies,' were everywhere; some estimates place the number of speakeasies in the city of New York alone at 100,000.

Aside from failing to curtail alcohol consumption, prohibition had additional, unintended consequences. Manufacture and sale of alcohol was legal in both Canada and Mexico, along with the island nations of the Caribbean; all that was required were people willing to smuggle the contraband into the country. This era would mark the rise of organized crime in the United States, where gangs used the opportunity to grow rich moving liquor into the United States, particularly across the Detroit River into the city of Chicago, where organized crime remains a major player, despite the repeal of prohibition nearly 80 years ago. With this smuggling activity came increased violence and political corruption, as gangs used whatever means necessary to fulfill the demand for alcohol in the States.

By the early 1930's, the public had grown weary of prohibition. The majority of people in the U.S. were drinkers, and the promised societal benefits of a temperate society had not come to fruition; instead Americans were facing increased organized crime, political corruption, and laws that were frequently ignored, often blatantly. The Great Depression, which had a devastating effect not only on individuals, but government coffers, offered the perfect excuse for repeal. Not only would re-opening breweries, wineries, and distilleries provide job opportunities, but the tax revenue would assist the cash-strapped federal government. In 1933, the twenty-first amendment would repeal the eighteenth, marking the first and only time that a constitutional amendment would be repealed; fitting for the only time the amendment process was used to add a restriction on personal liberty to a document originally intended to restrict government excess.

### *The Sedition Act of 1918*

In April 1917, in a response to continued attacks by German submarines against United States merchant shipping, the United States entered World War I by declaring war against Germany. During this period, the Wilson administration and members of Congress became increasingly worried about citizens acting disloyally to the United States, and on June 15, 1917, the Espionage Act was implemented. This Act made it a crime to interfere with military operations, materially support enemies during wartime, or to promote insubordination within the military or interfere with recruiting efforts.

However, in 1918, it was determined that merely outlawing material support for the enemy was not enough, and it was in the United States' best interest to outlaw even vocal disapproval of government actions. The resulting legislation, known as the Sedition Act, was an amendment to the Espionage Act, and it made it a federal crime to speak out against the government during wartime. Since the Act became law only six months before the end of hostilities, prosecutions were few, but those that did go to court and resulted in convictions carried prison sentences of five to twenty years. One such prosecution was that of seventy-year-old railroad executive and naturalized German immigrant William Edenborn, who was arrested following a speech in which he claimed the military threat from Germany was being exaggerated by the United States government. The offending excerpt from this speech was reprinted in the April 28, 1918 edition of the New York Times as follows[24]:

---

[24] A PDF copy of this story is available through the New York Times website at: http://query.nytimes.com/mem/archive-free/pdf?res=F20E11F9345B11738DDDA00A94DC405B888DF1D3

"There has been much talk about Germany coming over here and attacking the United States. We need have no fear that Germany will ever attack the United States. It would take a maritime nation to do that, because America is surrounded by water. America can look to other countries for any attacks in the future. Recently a certain prime minister stated, 'Our nation is mistress of the sea, our nation has been mistress of the sea, and always will be mistress of the sea.'"

The charge, reported in the same New York Times story, was that Edenborn's speech intended "to breathe the arrogant spirit of Prussianism in its most hateful form and amounts to seditious treason, being in effect pro-German propaganda of the most cunning, insidious, and demoralizing sort to the morale of the American people, having the direct effect of sowing seeds of discord, discontent, and hatred against a great government with whom we are associated in bonds of brotherly love." The point of Edenborn's statement was that Germany lacked the naval power to be a significant threat to the United States, and it would need to look elsewhere, to a nation with a significant naval history and presence, to find a true threat. He then quotes "a certain prime minister" – the Prime Minister of England, to be precise, as stating that they had a significant naval history and presence, the implication being that the United States had far more to fear from Great Britain than from Germany. Surely, such a statement, particularly during a war in which the United States and Great Britain were allied against Germany, was ill-advised; however, it is hard to justify the government's statement that his words were treasonous, or really anything more than the grumblings of an old man finding himself in a time where his adopted homeland was at war with his native homeland. Nevertheless, for the above statement, Edenborn was tried and convicted of sedition and spent time in a federal penitentiary.

Proponents of the Sedition Act, when they weren't issuing clearly inflammatory statements intended to defend trumped-up charges against septuagenarian businessmen, were defending the Act using what can only be described as tortured logic. One of the problems during the United States' involvement in World War I was the frequency with which acts of violence were perpetrated against war dissenters by those who considered themselves true patriots. These acts of violence, which were on the verge of becoming riots in some cases, required swift action. However, rather than prosecuting individuals for acts of violence and vandalism at the state and local level, the federal government decided that it was necessary to step in and take control of the situation. Of course, instead of stepping in to protect free speech rights, as required by the First Amendment, the government decided to make politically inconvenient speech illegal. This way, those true patriots wouldn't have anything to get so worked up over.

This solution to the issue has two very significant problems. First, on a philosophical level, it rewards bad behavior. The way the Sedition Act addresses its target problem is very much like solving the problem of violent racism by making it illegal to be non-white.

The second significant problem is that the law was clearly illegal. The First Amendment to the Constitution reads "Congress shall make no law respecting an establishment of religion, or prohibiting the free exercise thereof; **or abridging the freedom of speech**, or of the press; or the right of the people peaceably to assemble, and to petition the Government for a redress of grievances." (Emphasis added). While Supreme Court cases, such as

*Schenck v. United States* have held that the government can limit speech when such speech presents a 'clear and present danger' to national security, the Constitution has no such language; it has been added over the years by justices who find it convenient to expand federal power. Additionally, it is quite clear that speech such as Edenborn's represented no threat to national security at all. In fact, it was political speech, among other kinds of speech inconvenient to those in power, that the First Amendment was *specifically* designed to protect. The British, after all, had taken exception to such writings as Thomas Paine's *Common Sense*, and the founders had believed that disagreement with official government policy was something to be protected. After all, if the Bill of Rights is not intended to protect actions that are politically or socially inconvenient, then why bother protecting them at all? Saying something that is perfectly in line with the status quo is not something in need of legal protection; it is that which challenges the status quo that needs legal coverage.

### *Results of the Progressive Era*

The Progressive Era officially spanned the thirty years from 1890-1920. During this time, the federal government gained even more power through implementation of regulations on private industry, and much of this power was shifted from the Legislative branch to the Executive through the advent of administrative rule-making and expansion of the executive bureaucracy. This era would see the creation of the Departments of Labor and Commerce, which today employ more than 60,000 bureaucrats and spend more than $200 billion in tax dollars annually in pursuits outside of the federal government's original constitutional mandate. The government would also be expanded through the establishment of the Federal Reserve. However, this expansion in federal power was not, as many are led to believe, at the expense of big business, but in its interests. By exploiting manufactured crises, the federal government and giants in banking, manufacturing, oil, and transportation joined together in cartels which gave government more power and protected business from competition at the expense of individual liberty.

Individual liberty also took a hit in the form of the Sedition Act, which made it a crime to publicly criticize the government during wartime. This limitation on political speech set a dangerous precedent, and is one of the clearest examples of the federal government ignoring the protections of the Bill of Rights in favor of political expediency. That it was tolerated by the public at large shows that the public has evolved along a path inverse to the federal government – as the government's power has grown, the individual has accepted that his role must shrink.

The results of the Progressive Era are easily seen in the numbers. In 1921, when President Woodrow Wilson left office, the unemployment rate was 20%, and the policies of the Federal Reserve had caused 102% inflation since its founding in 1913. The American standard of living was significantly lower than it was at the start of the Progressive Era, and there was a national debt of $293 billion (in 2011 dollars). These results should not come as any surprise; the same results have been seen every time progressivism takes hold in the United States, as will be seen in the next chapter.

# Six

# The New Deal

*"The New Deal is plainly an attempt to achieve a working socialism and avert a social collapse in America; it is extraordinarily parallel to the successive 'policies' and 'Plans' of the Russian experiment. Americans shirk the word 'socialism', but what else can one call it?"*
H.G. Wells

In October of 1929, after nearly a decade of economic growth, the value of the U.S. stock market experienced a record collapse. On October 28, the market lost nearly 13% of its value, and the following day, it lost nearly 12%. According to the official narrative, this calamity was the result of the capitalistic greed of the 'roaring twenties' and an introduction to what would become a decade-long economic depression, requiring extraordinary intervention by the federal government to save the nation. Once again, this received wisdom is proven to be false when subjected to critical analysis, and the extraordinary measures taken by the central government are revealed for what they really are: attempts to exploit a crisis with the goal of accumulating additional power for the ruling class. By the time that the Great Depression was over, a central government that had spent 150 years consolidating power through coercion, violence, and manipulation of public opinion would have established itself not only as the supreme authority, but the supreme provider, through the establishment of such programs as Social Security and Medicare.

### *The 1929 Market Crash and Reaction*

In direct contradiction to the Progressive Era that was in effect during the first 20 years of the new century, the 1920's, under the presidency of Calvin Coolidge, could best be described as hands-off. Coolidge understood that the best way for government to stimulate economic activity was to get out of the way, which he did. During the Coolidge administration, income taxes were cut drastically (the top marginal rate was cut from 75% to 25%), and the regulatory apparatus, which had ballooned under his Progressive predecessors, was led by Coolidge appointees who understood that the President preferred that they do very little, and that much only if they could not get by with doing nothing at all.

In addition to promoting lower taxes and stalling the regulatory bureaucracy, Coolidge adamantly opposed farm subsidies and federal involvement in flood mitigation in the Mississippi River Basin. Himself a child of farm owners, he believed that farmers should be responsible for their own profits and that the states and individual land owners be responsible for their own flood mitigation efforts. His minimalist beliefs in taxes and federal involvement were coupled with a belief that the federal government should spend less money; federal budgets were lowered considerably during his tenure, and the federal debt was nearly halved by the time he left office.

Overall, Coolidge's presidency may be the closest to that envisioned by the founders since that generation died off. Coolidge did not see the federal government as the peoples' provider, or their conscience; he believed that taxation was immoral, and that people should take care of themselves.

The results of this change in federal executive policy were staggering. By the time that Coolidge left office in 1929, the unemployment rate, which had reached nearly 20% at the end of the Progressive Era, was cut to 3.2% in 1929. Additionally, federal debt, as a percent of gross domestic product, was cut from nearly 30% in 1920 to just over 16% in 1929. This dramatic turnaround should have served as undeniable proof that the best government policy was to stay out of the way. Unfortunately, this was not to be the case.

During the presidential elections of 1928, one of the hot topics was that of trade tariffs. Republican Herbert Hoover, who had served as Secretary of Commerce under Coolidge and was now campaigning to follow him as President, supported farm tariffs, but wanted to leave industrial tariffs low. After his victory, and election results that left comfortable Republican majorities in both houses of Congress, Hoover asked Congress for an increase in Agricultural tariffs. Congress responded with the Smoot-Hawley Tariff Act. Sponsored by Reed Smoot, a Republican from Utah and Chairman of the Senate Finance Committee, and Willis Hawley, a Republican from Oregon, the bill increased both agricultural and industrial tariffs to near record levels. The only time in American history that tariffs had been raised higher than those proposed by

Smoot-Hawley was in 1828, under the Tariff of Abominations, which was a direct cause of the secession of seven states in 1860-1861. In light of this, the idea that the Smoot-Hawley Tariff Act would result in domestic unrest and economic calamity should not have been a surprise. In fact, 1,028 economists signed a letter to Hoover advising him not to sign the act, and J.P. Morgan and Henry Ford, two of the titans of American industry the Act was ostensibly written to favor, personally pleaded with the new president to veto it, fearing retaliation from foreign governments. Hoover, who had publicly criticized the bill, nevertheless bowed to pressure from his own party and signed Smoot-Hawley into law on June 17, 1930.

While the Act was not signed into law until mid-1930, the response began much earlier, even before Hoover's election. While campaigning for President in 1928, Hoover had voiced support for an increase in tariffs, as had Republicans campaigning for legislative seats. Once the new President and his Republican colleagues in Congress took office in 1929, serious work on the tariff began.

Not surprisingly, America's foreign trading partners were not pleased at the prospect of these tariffs. Twenty-three U.S. trading partners sent formal protest letters to Washington, and Canada, the United States' largest trading partner, preemptively increased tariffs on U.S. goods while shifting significant amounts of imports to the United Kingdom.

Though Washington viewed the international developments with the kind of perceptiveness the federal government has become famous for, Wall Street was keenly aware of the damage that the proposed tariff posed for international business. Even though exports only accounted for about 5% of GDP in 1929, it was enough to make investors very nervous, and when investors began to pull out of the market in October 1929 in the face of an almost assured Hoover victory, it triggered a massive panic and sell-off, which peaked on Thursday, October 24. Following the collapse on the 24th, stocks continued to decline into mid-November.

At this point, investor confidence had been deeply shaken, and this uncertainty would spread into the public at large. However, the economic damage to the nation was not as bad as many believe; only 16% of Americans were invested in the market, which is a much smaller percentage than today. The fact that the market collapse occurred during the downswing of a normal economic oscillatory period was unfortunate, but the entire episode would likely have ended in nothing worse than a moderate-to-severe recession, with a normal recovery, had the federal government not stepped in to try and fix it.

First, even though the mere debate on the bill proved poisonous to the market, the Smoot-Hawley Tariff Act was passed by Congress and signed by President Hoover in 1930. This move resulted in the expected retaliatory tariffs from U.S. trade partners and further damage to the market.

Second, the Federal Reserve Bank reversed the monetary policy that had been in effect for an entire decade almost overnight. Throughout the 1920's, the Fed had maintained a monetary policy where credit was easy, and currency was not tied to real goods or assets. This move was made to maintain the status quo with European powers, who had abandoned real asset backing for their currency in the aftermath of the First World War in an attempt to salvage their devastated economies. This policy had the benefit of providing price stability for consumers, and may have helped contribute to the economic boom of the 1920's.

However, following the death of Federal Reserve chairman Benjamin Strong in 1928, the Federal Reserve quickly shifted to a Real Bills doctrine, which required that all currency in circulation be backed by material goods. Because the monetary policy of the 1920's had not required such backing, the Federal Reserve had issued far more currency than they had material goods to cover; as a result, the change to a real bills policy required that 30% of the nation's currency be taken out of circulation. The resulting deflation could not have occurred at a worse time, and severely crippled the nation's ability to recover from the worsening depression.

This is not to say that the monetary policy of the 1920's was correct. In fact, had the Federal Reserve maintained a real bills policy instead of abandoning it following World War I, and maintained realistic credit policies, it is very likely that the resulting monetary stability would have prevented the recession at the end of the 1920's from turning into a depression, although at the cost of some of the 1920's prosperity. Nobel prize-winning economist Friedrich Hayek predicted the American market crash from London earlier in 1929[25]:

> "I was one of the only ones to predict what was going to happen. In early 1929, when I made this forecast, I was living in Europe which was then going through a period of depression. I said that there [would be] no hope of a recovery in Europe until interest rates fell, and interest rates would not fall until the American boom collapses, which I said was likely to happen within the next few months."

---

[25] From a June, 1975 interview with Monex International's *Gold & Silver Newsletter*.

However, while Hayek disagreed with the monetary policy of the 1920's, he also believed that the response to the crash was equally faulty. From a 1979 interview:

> "I agree with Milton Friedman that once the Crash had occurred, the Federal Reserve System pursued a silly deflationary policy. I am not only against inflation but I am also against deflation. So, once again, a badly programmed monetary policy prolonged the depression."

It seems that the easy credit policies of the 1920's were at least partly to blame for the economic downturn, but the rush to correct this problem only made matters worse. Perhaps the best lesson to learn from this is that having a quasi-governmental entity that has the power to centrally plan the monetary policy for the nation is a bad idea.

In addition to poor monetary policy and bad trade regulation, Hoover decided to damage the economy even further by raising income taxes. In 1932, Hoover signed the Revenue Act of 1932, which was the largest peacetime tax increase in American history, raising the top marginal rate from 25% to 63%. This rate would be increased to 79% during Franklin Roosevelt's first term, along with other increases in personal and corporate income tax rates.

There are, of course, additional reasons for the recession of the late 1920's and the depression that followed. The settlement actions taken at the end of World War I, a slowdown in population growth resulting from World War I casualties and deaths from the 1918 Spanish Flu epidemic, and the reduction in labor demand resulting from widespread automation in manufacturing all played a part. However, it is clear that the government's actions during the crisis amplified and prolonged its effect.

Throughout American history, and as outlined in this book, it is clear that the federal government, created by the founders to provide the individual states with common defense and shared economic ties, has used any opportunity available to expand its power over both the states and its individual citizens. Furthermore, when the situations allowing it to naturally assume more power have not presented themselves, it has taken steps to initiate those situations. Therefore, it should come as no surprise that a mere decade after the interventionist policies of the Progressive Era devastated the economy, and immediately following an era in which a hands-off approach had seen the economy soar, the government chose to exploit an economic downturn as an opportunity to seize control. It was not enough that central planning had made the crisis worse; as is seen repeatedly in American history, there is no government-created problem that the government cannot promise to correct through further government intervention.

### A 'New Deal' is Promised

Herbert Hoover was rightly blamed for much of the nation's economic situation. Although he did not act alone, fellow Republicans controlled the legislative branch, and Hoover served as a partially-culpable scapegoat. It was no surprise, therefore, that he was soundly defeated in 1932 by Franklin Delano Roosevelt, a Democrat and cousin of Progressive-era president Theodore Roosevelt. What is interesting, however, is the platform upon which Roosevelt won. A decade earlier, Calvin Coolidge had led the nation through a government-caused financial crisis by getting out of the way and letting the market correct itself, with very positive results. However, Franklin Roosevelt promoted an economic policy to combat the Great

Depression heavily influenced by John Maynard Keynes, who had published his *Treatise on Money* two years earlier. Keynes, one of the most influential economists of the 20th Century, argued that government planning, not free markets, was the solution to weak economies, and that governments could spend enough money to jump-start economic activity in the private sector. He even advocated heavy deficit spending, concluding that the resultant increase in economic activity would create revenues sufficient to pay off the debt incurred. Roosevelt therefore proposed a massive list of government-funded public works and stimulus projects, including the Civilian Conservation Corps, the Federal Emergency Relief Act, and the Tennessee Valley Authority Act. All of these provided massive amounts of federal money to fund infrastructure projects, with the idea that workers would be hired to complete those projects. This ambitious platform, which would put the federal government back on the Progressive track, was effectively the opposite of Coolidge's strategy. Since Coolidge's strategy was wildly successful, it is unclear why the electorate believed such an activist intervention was advisable; nevertheless, as will be seen, Roosevelt's reaction to the Great Depression could not have been worse, and lengthened the crisis by a number of years.

### *Economic Changes*

In addition to massive stimulus spending, Roosevelt proposed, and Congress enacted, a number of changes to the U.S. economic system. In the banking sector, the Emergency Banking Act of 1933 effectively placed the entire banking industry under the control of the President and the Federal Reserve Bank. Among its stipulations were that, upon declaration of a national emergency, the President could take complete control over national finances, that during such an emergency, all banking activity would be illegal unless approved by the President, and allowed the Comptroller of the Currency to take control of and establish its administrative terms. The Act also authorized the Treasury Department to seize all privately held gold in exchange for U.S. currency. In 1935, the Glass-Steagall Act would establish the Federal Depository Insurance Corporation (FDIC), a new bureaucracy that would insure bank depositors for up to $5000 per account.

In addition to taking control of the banking industry, Roosevelt's policies also included the abandonment of the gold standard. Prior to 1933, all United States currency could, by law, be exchanged for its worth in gold. The gold standard was adopted for a number of reasons; gold backing provided stability in the international market, resulting in less fluctuation in exchange rates, and it protected against inflation, since the government could not flood the market with paper currency it did not have backing for. As discussed earlier, one of the causes of the Great Depression was conflicting monetary policy, which resulted in expansion of the money supply in the 1920's and quick contraction of the supply at the end of the decade. An abandonment of the gold standard signaled that the Federal Reserve did not learn its lesson from this incident, and instead wanted unfettered ability to inflate currency to help pay for all of the government stimulus.

The Agricultural Adjustment Act, passed May 12 1933, became an early form of agricultural welfare. Crop production methods had increased dramatically during the 1920's, and farmers enjoyed high crop prices since much of what was grown in the United States was shipped to a Europe still attempting to recover from the first World

War. However, as Europe recovered its own agricultural capability in the late 1920's, the reduction in exports caused a surge in food commodity availability, and resulted in a sharp decline in crop prices. In response, the AAA authorized the federal government to pay farmers not to grow crops. Government funding paid for 10 million acres of crops to be plowed under and 6 million pigs to be slaughtered and the meat destroyed, amongst other government-sponsored food destruction and prevention measures aimed at keeping food commodity prices artificially high. Although declared unconstitutional in 1936, the AAA was modified to satisfy the Supreme Court's objections without significant changes. Ironically, the purpose of the AAA shifted in 1934 to assisting farmers displaced by the Dust Bowl, and then at the start of World War II to assisting farmers to increase crop production to meet war needs. Therefore, in the course of a single decade, a single government program went from giving farmers money to not grow crops to giving farmers money to recover from planting too many crops, to giving money to farmers to increase crop production.

### *Labor Reforms*

The New Deal would also focus on one of the Progressive Era's pet topics: labor. While the Progressive Era made changes to workplace safety laws, the New Deal would focus more on how long an employee worked each week, how much he would be paid, and the legalities of organizing labor. To this end, the National Industrial Recovery Act (NIRA) was passed in 1933. The NIRA allowed workers to form and join unions and enter into collective bargaining contracts, and allowed the President to impose a minimum wage and maximum working hours.

The NIRA also empowered the President to exempt companies from federal antitrust laws if he determined that the operation of the monopoly was in the nation's best interests.

The NIRA, like much of the New Deal legislation, led to the creation of more federal bureaucracy. In this case, it was not one, but two federal agencies: the National Recovery Administration (NRA), and the Public Works Administration (PWA). The Act also provided a budget of $400 million ($6.5 billion in 2011 dollars) to be spent on public infrastructure projects, which were designed to boost employment numbers.

The sweeping powers provided to the Executive branch by the NIRA were met with constitutional challenges and in May 1935, Title I of the Act, which gave the President code making powers and allowed him to exempt businesses from antitrust laws, was declared unconstitutional in the case of *A.L.A. Schechter Poultry v. United States*. From Chief Justice Charles Hughes' opinion:

> "In view of the scope of that broad declaration and of the nature of the few restrictions that are imposed, the discretion of the President in approving or prescribing codes, and thus enacting laws for the government of trade and industry throughout the country, is virtually unfettered. We think that the code-making authority thus conferred is an unconstitutional delegation of legislative power."

### *Economic Results of New Deal Programs*

One of the things that is remarkably clear when considering the New Deal stimulus and investment programs is how different this approach was from that taken by President Coolidge in the 1920's. Instead of Coolidge's hands-off approach, Hoover and Roosevelt were determined to fix the economy by force. That Hoover's approach was so far removed from Coolidge's, in whose cabinet he had served, should come as no surprise; Hoover had been a holdover from Warren Harding's administration that Coolidge had never bothered to replace, since he did not see the Secretary of Commerce to be a particularly important posting. Coolidge even went on the record as being at odds with Hoover when it came to economic policy, once saying of Hoover, "for six years that man has given me unsolicited advice—all of it bad." Franklin Roosevelt would continue policies similar to Hoover's, only more extreme. Billions of dollars were sunk into stimulus projects and programs intended to artificially modify prices away from market stability points, and the labor reforms that Roosevelt sold to the nation under the guise of fairness and equality raised the costs of employing workers to a point that many employers could not afford, resulting in an extended period of high unemployment. In fact, there were fewer individuals employed by the private sector in 1940 than there were in 1929, despite an increase in the work-age population and thousands of pages of legislation and regulation designed to 'fix' the unemployment problem. In the midst of it all, however, millions of new jobs were created in various government agencies and stimulus programs administering those regulations.

In 2004, economists at the University of California at Los Angeles attempted to quantify the damage that Roosevelt did to the economy through his combination of stimulus, bureaucracy, and regulation. According to Professor of Economics Harold L. Cole[26],

"President Roosevelt believed that excessive competition was responsible for the Depression by reducing prices and wages, and by extension reducing employment and demand for goods and services. So he came up with a recovery package that would be unimaginable today, allowing businesses in every industry to collude without the threat of antitrust prosecution and workers to demand salaries about 25 percent above where they ought to have been, given market forces. The economy was poised for a beautiful recovery, but that recovery was stalled by these misguided policies."

Fellow economics professor Lee E. Ohanian describes why these policies led to the continuation of economic problems:

"High wages and high prices in an economic slump run contrary to everything we know about market forces in economic downturns," Ohanian said. "As we've seen in the past several years, salaries and prices fall when unemployment is high. By artificially inflating both, the New Deal policies short-circuited the market's self-correcting forces."

Through an analysis of market indicators, Cole and Ohanian determined that the Great Depression officially ended in 1943, but calculate that had Roosevelt not intervened, even with the damage done by Hoover, the depression would have been over by 1936 – a full seven years earlier. For individuals who promote free-market

[26] From a February, 2009 Wall Street Journal Opinion piece: *How Government Prolonged the Depression*

economics, this is hardly a surprise; proponents of Adam Smith's free-market philosophy, including many of the nation's founders, believed that freedom was a moral good, and that therefore, any policy that supported such would meet with success. In his arrogance, Roosevelt believed that he knew better than the laws of God and nature; the result was an additional seven years of poverty for millions of Americans. Such poverty was the cause of the next topic; with so many out of work and starving as the result of federal policies, the federal government would have to step in once again to save the American people from a catastrophe that it had caused.

### *The Welfare State*

As with most of the responsibilities which the national government has taken on since its inception, the method for caring for the poor was intended by the Constitution's writers to be addressed by the states. It should also be noted that it is perfectly constitutional for any given state's method of caring for the poor to be to allow private charity to handle things. There is nothing in the United States constitution requiring either the federal or state governments to provide public assistance. However, the idea of public assistance is nothing new. As early as 1535, the English Poor Laws provided assistance both for those unable to work due to age or disability as well as those able to work but unable to find employment. As with much of the social structure imported from Great Britain, various versions of the poor laws existed in the states from before the Revolutionary War and up until the Great Depression. Generally, these laws provided monetary handouts to those unable to work, but the able-bodied were required to admit themselves to a workhouse in order to receive aid. Workhouses were institutions which provided food and housing for individuals and families that were unable to support themselves. In exchange for lodging at a workhouse, boarders were expected to work, typically at menial jobs. In this system, local taxation funded programs for taking care of the poor, and all support was administered locally.

Of course, government assistance was not the only source of care for those unable to care for themselves. Private charity, including charity from wealthy individuals and religious institutions, helped those unable to care for themselves. In fact, the Pennsylvania Hospital, the first hospital in the United States, was started by Dr. Thomas Bond and founding father Benjamin Franklin as a way to care for the poor sick and insane of Philadelphia. This hospital operated on private funds, supplied by wealthy concerned citizens, without government compulsion or administration.

However, in 1935, it was determined that these locally administered programs were no longer sufficient, and federal intervention was necessary to alleviate the poverty inflicted by the Great Depression, itself a result of federal policy. Some of the proposed methods for implementing this change were extremely radical. According to the Social Security Administration[27]:

> "Huey Long was Governor of Louisiana from 1928 to 1932 and was elected to the U.S. Senate in 1930. A nominal Democrat, Huey Long was a radical populist. He wanted the government to confiscate the wealth of the nation's rich and privileged. He called his program Share Our Wealth. It called upon the federal government to guarantee every

---

[27] From Long's Social Security Online bio:
http://www.ssa.gov/history/hlong1.html

family in the nation an annual income of $5,000, so they could have the necessities of life, including a home, a job, a radio and an automobile. He also proposed limiting private fortunes to $50 million, legacies to $5 million, and annual incomes to $1 million. Everyone over age 60 would receive an old-age pension. His slogan was 'Every Man A King'."

Clearly, Long's position more closely matches that of Karl Marx than that of the United States' founders. To limit personal income and wealth and to agitate for government seizure of personal property deemed excessive is directly contradictory to the United States' original principles, primary among which was the idea that personal property, when acquired legally, is inviolable. According to John Locke, "Government has no other end, but the preservation of property." It was, in fact, government confiscation of private property without due process and proper representation that led to the Declaration of Independence, the Revolutionary War, and the American experiment itself. This kind of behavior is frequently represented in human history; principles are all well and good when things are running smoothly, but the moment that problems occur, principle is abandoned in a rush to 'do something' to address the crisis. The irony of this situation is that if the principles are sound, the crisis itself is usually the result of failure to abide by the principles in the first place. Clearly this conclusion can be drawn from the Great Depression and subsequent reaction.

Another interesting point to note in Huey Long's platform is the expansion of the definition of 'necessity' – the original Poor Laws had provided for food and shelter, but Long expanded necessities to include a home (presumably meaning a dwelling where families would live separate from other families), a radio, and a car. This shift in what is considered a necessity would influence welfare programs from this point forward.

While Long's "Every Man a King" proposal would not come to fruition, it would not entirely die, either. Ultimately, the programs developed by the federal government would be much closer to Long's, and, therefore, Marx's, ideas than those of the nation's founders. The first result of this change in public assistance was the Social Security Act of 1935, which provided old-age assistance to those in need, as well as the first national unemployment insurance plan. To those familiar with the Social Security system of the 21st Century, there is an interesting requirement in the Act which has been abandoned: the original Act required the Secretary of the Treasury to "invest such portion of the amounts credited to the Account as is not, in his judgment, required to meet current withdrawals. Such investment may be made only in interest-bearing obligations of the United States or in obligations guaranteed as to both principal and interest by the United States." Today, there is no Account. All funds contributed to Social Security via payroll taxes are immediately transferred to the United States General Fund and spent. While this provision does not make the Social Security system any more constitutional, it certainly would have made it more fiscally sound, provided that it was allowed to remain in effect. The fact that it was abandoned instead manages to demonstrate that federal programs, even those intended to assist those in need, become less fiscally sound, and therefore a greater drain on society at large, the longer they are allowed to persist.

The cost of Social Security has expanded dramatically since 1935, due both to expansions in the program which were part of President Lyndon Johnson's 'Great Society' programs of the 1960's, and also due to a vast expansion in the number of Americans living to receive benefits, and the amount of time that those receiving benefits remained alive to receive them. In order to understand this expansion, it is important to understand the initial intent of the program. Social Security was originally intended as a social insurance program. As with most insurance programs, it was meant to protect against an event which may or may not occur; in this case reaching an age where it was no longer possible to work. In 1940 for example, 54% of men and 60% of women who reached adulthood (21 years) would live to the age of 65. Those that did reach this age were expected to live an additional 14.7 years (men) or 16.7 years (women). In 1990, 72.3% of men and 83.6% of women who reached adulthood were expected to live to 65, and the life expectancy for those reaching 65 was extended by an additional 4 years. This means that, due to improvements in living conditions and medical technology, living to 65 is no longer an achievement, and those living to 65 are generally much more physically able. The logical result of this increase in both physical ability and life expectancy in light of Social Security as an insurance program would be to expect people to work longer. After all, the original intent of Social Security was not to entitle people to retirement, but to provide a minimal income in the event that old age prevented them from working before they died. The problem is that Social Security is no longer seen as an insurance program protecting against old-age frailty, but an entitlement. Americans have become accustomed to the idea that they are entitled to retire at 65, and live another two decades without working. While it is unquestionably nice to spend the twilight years resting rather than working, this attitude has placed a great strain on the American economy; in 2011, 20% of federal expenditures were tied directly to Social Security payments, and the program now pays more in benefits than it takes in from payroll taxes. Furthermore, since the fund which was originally established to invest payroll taxes for workers has been abandoned, it means that current workers are being taxed to pay benefits for those currently receiving them, making Social Security not only fiscally unsound, but the largest Ponzi scheme in history.

In addition to the economic problems that Social Security poses, there are constitutional concerns as well. In fact, the authors of the 1935 Act believed that it was unconstitutional. Thomas H. Eliot, who served as counsel for the Committee on Economic Security, which developed the Social Security Act, knew that it would not stand up to strict constitutional scrutiny. In a 1961 speech, he had this to say[28]:

> "The opponents rallied as soon as the bill was introduced. Those opponents were spearheaded by the U.S. Chamber of Commerce and the National Association of Manufacturers. Counsel for the latter, John Gall, made effective and strong arguments against that phase of the bill (old-age insurance). He questioned the constitutionality of the bill.

> "These arguments I found rather difficult to refute, and I'm glad I wasn't really called upon to do so as a witness before the committees of Congress because I had very grave doubts at that time about the likelihood of the Court's upholding the old-age insurance section of the bill."

---

[28] In a speech to the Social Security Administration

Edwin E. Witte, Roosevelt's Executive Director for the Committee on Economic Security, agreed with Eliot. In a 1955 speech, he also stated that most of those involved with Social Security, including those who voted for it, believed it unconstitutional[29]:

> "A majority of the members of the Senate Committee on Finance believed old-age insurance to be unconstitutional," said Witte, "and it is my belief that several voted for it in the expectation that it would be invalidated by the Supreme Court."

Such sentiment was of course not limited to Social Security; many of Roosevelt's New Deal programs had been declared unconstitutional, and many more were in fact unconstitutional but had managed to stand, probably as a result of the massive growth of federal jurisdiction that had occurred through the previous century. However, the frequent constitutional challenges to the New Deal presented a problem for men like Roosevelt, who wished to completely reshape the country. A solution for this nuisance would have to be found.

### *Packing the Courts*

Throughout his first term, President Roosevelt attempted to completely reshape the American economic system. While corporate favoritism and legislation designed to guide the market in particular directions goes back to Washington's first term, FDR seemed intent on transforming the United States into a completely centrally planned socialist economy with almost completely

---

[29] From a 1955 speech commemorating the 20th anniversary of the bill.

unchecked executive authority. Every major piece of New Deal legislation contained language giving unprecedented authority to the President to unilaterally regulate, enforce, and control the private sector.

Roosevelt ran into a problem, however. While a tremendous amount of legislation had been developed and passed during his first term, much of it had been declared unconstitutional, and as has already been seen, that which wasn't declared unconstitutional probably would not have held up under scrutiny if it had been subjected to a significant legal challenge. Proponents of the New Deal understood that they were trying to turn America into something that was not within the bounds of the Constitution, and needed to ensure that future legislation would be allowed to pass constitutional muster.

The legitimate way to accomplish this would have been to amend the Constitution to allow increased federal powers and move what had previously been legislative authority to the executive branch. After all, if the constitution is amended to allow something, it can hardly be called unconstitutional. Prior to Roosevelt, this seemed to be understood; for all the damage that the Progressive Era did to the nation's founding principles, at least some of the changes made to American government had been accomplished through the amendment process; a total of four constitutional amendments were ratified in the decade between 1909 and 1919. In contrast, despite the dramatic changes to be attempted during the New Deal, the only constitutional amendment to be enacted was in the first year of Roosevelt's first term, which repealed Prohibition in an attempt to increase economic activity.

Instead of attempting to amend the Constitution, Roosevelt chose another tactic – he attempted to reconfigure the Supreme Court so that he would be allowed to ignore it. In 1937, Roosevelt proposed the Judicial

Procedures Reform Bill, which would have allowed him to add an additional Supreme Court justice for every sitting justice over the age of 70. The argument for this bill was that the Court needed additional justices in order to keep current on cases; this argument was clearly disingenuous, and was demonstrated to be so by the court, which was at the time the legislation was proposed completely up-to-date on its case load. The real reason for the bill was of course to allow Roosevelt and his conspirators in the Senate to pack the court with justices sympathetic to the New Deal and willing to allow the government to circumvent constitutional authority. The public recognized the attempt for what it was, and the Bill was scuttled under public pressure, but not without having its intended effect; following the introduction of the bill, the Supreme Court would not declare another piece of New Deal legislation unconstitutional, a reversal seen by many as a recognition by the sitting justices that the court was vulnerable to executive tampering, should its decisions become too inconvenient to the President.

### Gun Control Becomes a Federal Issue

By the time of the New Deal, the federal government had already demonstrated that it had no problems infringing on the First Amendment rights of citizens; the Sedition Act made some political speech illegal, in direct contradiction of the intent of the Bill of Rights. During Franklin Roosevelt's administration, the federal government would continue this trend by taking aim at the Second Amendment, which forbade the federal government from placing limitations on American's right to bear arms.

The justification for federal gun control would come as the result of another federal action – prohibition. As already detailed, the outlaw of alcohol in the United States had created a surge in organized crime, which gained wealth and power by smuggling liquor into the U.S. from Canada, Mexico, and the Caribbean. Mobsters had no moral qualms with engaging in armed combat with law enforcement, and their weapons of choice, the Thompson .45 machine gun and Browning Automatic Rifle, were military weapons that were completely legal for private citizens to own. In 1934 Congress passed, and Roosevelt signed, the National Firearms Act, which did not outlaw these weapons, but placed a heavy tax on them and mandated federal registration. Gangsters, of course, responded by ignoring these laws just as they had ignored liquor laws.

While prior to 1934 gun rights had been considered inviolable, the National Firearms Act cleared the way for the federal government to increasingly regulate firearms sales and ownership. Through the decades, seven additional federal laws have been passed restricting who is allowed to own a firearm, who is allowed to sell firearms, and what firearms can be sold and owned. While gun control advocates argue that such restrictions are necessary for public safety, these arguments face two problems. First, studies show that gun control efforts not only do not prevent violent crime, but increases in gun ownership actually serve to prevent such crime. Second, gun control at the federal level is illegal according to the Second Amendment. The fact that such laws are allowed to be passed and enforced is yet another demonstration that the federal government has no respect for the rule of law and believes it can do anything that it wants.

## Executive Order 9066

Economic crisis was the primary excuse for the expansion of federal authority during Roosevelt's presidency, but as with all of American history, there is another event which is used to justify the expansion of governmental power and the limitation of personal liberty – war.

Following the Japanese attack on Pearl Harbor on December 7, 1941, public suspicion against both Japanese immigrants and American-born U.S. citizens of Japanese descent rose dramatically. In response, President Roosevelt issued Executive Order 9066 in May 1942, which allowed the Secretary of War and his subordinate military commanders to establish 'military areas' and exclude certain residents from such areas in the interest of national security. While the Order does not mention residents of Japanese ancestry directly, it was intended to remove anyone of Japanese descent from the west coast in an attempt to appease the public. Eventually, nearly a third of the United States would be declared a 'military area' and placed off-limits from those of Japanese descent. Approximately 110,000 Japanese-Americans were gathered up from these areas and relocated to internment camps, where they were held until the end of the war. These camps provided a poor standard of living, according to War Relocation Authority reports, lacking basic amenities such as indoor plumbing and proper cooking facilities. Additionally, those removed from the 'military areas' to internment camps were not allowed to take more than could be carried with them and as a result many of those interned came home several years later only to find that their personal property had been looted, and their homes had new occupants. For a government founded by those who believed government existed solely to protect personal liberty and private property, internment proved yet a new low.

Two Supreme Court challenges to internment were heard: the first was *Hirabayashi v. United States* in 1943 and the second was *Korematsu v. United States* in 1944. Both cases claimed that the United States government had violated the plaintiff's Fifth Amendment rights by denying due process. While a ruling in favor of the plaintiffs should have been obvious, in both cases, the Supreme Court sided with the government, arguing that matters of national security superseded the individual's rights. However, Korematsu's conviction was overturned in 1983 when it was demonstrated that the United States Solicitor General withheld evidence that the government did not believe interned Japanese presented a significant threat to national security.

While the cancellation of Korematsu's conviction for failure to vacate a 'military area' and enter an internment camp is welcome, the fact that it hinged on the fact that the government did not legitimately believe him a threat to national security based solely on his ancestry is not nearly as encouraging. Korematsu filed his lawsuit on Fifth Amendment grounds, and this should have been more than enough to overturn the conviction, along with the entire relocation and internment scheme. The text of the Fifth Amendment is simple, and the so-called Due Process clause is even simpler. In total, the clause reads, "No person shall be... deprived of life, liberty, or property, without due process of law..." There is no caveat in the Constitution that allows these rights to be suspended during time of war; in fact, it should be understood that protection of these rights was specifically enumerated to be protected during times of national stress, since these were the times when they were most likely to be abridged. Even

Tom C. Clark, who served as counsel for the U.S. Justice Department during the relocation before serving on the Supreme Court himself, recognized the unconstitutionality of the relocation. From the epilogue of the book *Executive Order 9066: The Internment of 110,000 Japanese Americans*:

> "The truth is, the writ of habeas corpus shall not be suspended, and despite the Fifth Amendment's command that no person shall be deprived of life, liberty or property without due process of law, both of these constitutional safeguards were denied by military action under Executive Order 9066."

### *Consequences of FDR and the New Deal*

Franklin Delano Roosevelt's presidency caused irreparable damage to both the Constitution and American life in general. Throughout his presidency, whether it was in response to economic woes or a surprise attack from a foreign nation, the reaction was the same: increased power given to the executive and restrictions on the liberty of private citizens. Furthermore, when attempts were made to limit these overreaches, Roosevelt responded with an attack plan intended to diminish the authority of the other government branches, specifically the Supreme Court. While many progressives idolize Roosevelt today, and he is credited with being the driving force behind both pulling the United States out of the Great Depression and winning the second World War, the truth is almost exactly opposite. Roosevelt's Keynesian policies extended both the duration and the magnitude of the Great Depression, his New Deal policies further centralized authority in the Executive Branch of the national government, and entitlements such as Social Security have created a financial burden that hangs around the neck of every modern American. Furthermore, the internment of Japanese-Americans (and to a lesser extent German- and Italian-Americans) by executive order, and the subsequent legal rationalization of this act by the Supreme Court shows that, much like a king, the president could order martial law and the effective imprisonment of American citizens without probable cause or due process, even though both are constitutional guarantees for every citizen. While the Sedition Act of 1918 had been a vile overreach of federal power, at least the law was passed by Congress and required the violator to actually do something, even if that something was Constitutionally-protected behavior. With Executive Order 9066, FDR managed to circumvent the legislative process completely and make national origin punishable by imprisonment. When Patrick Henry boycotted the Constitutional Convention in 1787 because he "smelt a rat in Philadelphia, tending toward the monarchy," it is easy to believe it was this kind of abuse of power he was warning against.

Finally, while the FDR years managed to trample the Constitution without bothering to go the legitimate route by amending it, Roosevelt's seemingly unquenchable thirst for power ironically resulted in a new Constitutional amendment; his refusal to follow George Washington's precedent and retire following two terms forced the United States to constitutionally limit any future presidency to two terms. This legacy is perhaps fitting for a man who clearly had no respect for the document.

# Seven

# The Post New Deal Welfare State

*"The government's view of the economy could be summed up in a few short phrases: If it moves, tax it. If it keeps moving, regulate it. And if it stops moving, subsidize it."*
Ronald Reagan

The years following the New Deal and FDR's presidency have greatly expanded the national government's role in American's lives, but only quantitatively, rather than qualitatively. Effectively, the idea of a federal system where state and national governments coexisted by exercising authority in equal but different spheres was a casualty of the Civil War. In this battle, the national authority won, and the states, which had previously operated as quasi-independent sovereign bodies, became much more like vassal states, implementing federal mandates as required and becoming increasingly reliant on federal funds to operate.

During the Progressive Era, the national government turned its attention to the private sector, implementing new regulations and oversight related to the private sector in an attempt to centrally manage the economy. Progressives also established a precedent of using federal authority to curtail individual liberty in an attempt to legislate moral behaviors. The Progressive Era also saw the start of the shift from a balance of power among the three branches of the federal government to a more powerful executive branch, via the implementation of executive rule-making.

Franklin Roosevelt's presidency would see the shift to executive dominance completed. Through intimidation and expansion of bureaucracy, FDR was able to exploit the dual crises of the Great Depression and World War II to give the President almost unlimited authority, including the ability to not only act where the Constitution did not give the federal government generally, or the President specifically, authority, but to act where the Constitution specifically prohibits action, as was seen with the internment of tens of thousands of Japanese-Americans following the attack on Pearl Harbor. When viewed with an eye for the rule of law and with the focus on personal liberty, the entirety of American history becomes one long slide from liberty and republic to authority and monarchy, and in many cases was cynically sold to the American public under the guise of greater democracy.

While the welfare state was instituted under FDR's careful watch, it was not the end of the growth of the welfare state; indeed, while the Social Security Act established precedence for Washington to act as provider for individual Americans, national welfare programs have expanded well beyond the 1935 act's initial ambitions, and today the full line-up of welfare and entitlement programs consumes the largest percentage of the national government's budget and threatens to completely bankrupt the nation.

### *The Great Society*

President Lyndon Johnson's 'War on Poverty' was sold as a great nation acting to rid itself of the affliction of the needy. In order to accomplish this task, Johnson was able to enact the largest slate of federal programs since the New Deal, beginning in 1964. The Department of Housing and Urban Development was established in 1965 to provide, among other things, financial assistance for housing to poor families. In a modification to the Social Security Act in 1965, Medicare was established to provide health care for the old and disabled, and Medicaid was established to provide health care for the poor. A number of educational programs were enacted, including Head Start, which provided preschool for poor children. The Job Corps was established, which provided vocational training for poor adults. The National Endowment of the Arts was created, which funneled taxpayer money to artists and galleries.

At this point, it is silly to question if any of the Great Society programs were Constitutional. Nothing in the document provided the federal government with the authority to regulate the housing market, provide health care, regulate education, provide vocational training, or fund artwork that could not survive on private funding. Nor is it prudent to ask if the programs in general at least promoted the founder's ideals of individual liberty, since the entire scheme relied on the confiscation of private property in the form of income taxes. Instead, it may be instructive to look at the results of these programs in order to determine if, while technically illegal, they were at least effective.

For those that believe that liberty and individual responsibility are the greatest moral good, and that freedom results in the greatest wealth for the greatest number of people, the answers are unsurprising. In total, Great Society programs have cost the United States more than $7 trillion since the mid-1960's. During that time, as economist Murray Rothbard points out[30]:

> "The plight of the inner cities is clearly worse than ever: more welfare, more crime, more dysfunction, more fatherless families, fewer kids being 'educated' in any sense, more despair and degradation.... It should be clear, in the starkest terms, that throwing taxpayer money and privileges at the inner cities is starkly counterproductive. And yet: this is the only 'solution' that liberals can ever come up with, and without any argument—as if this 'solution' were self-evident. How long is this nonsense supposed to go on?"

The numbers tend to support Rothbard's assertion. In 1964, when Johnson declared a war on poverty, the poverty rate in the United States was 19%. In the decades that have followed, the rate has never dropped below 11%, and in 2010 it was at 15%[31]. Therefore, it is easy to conclude that there has been nothing more than a marginal decrease in poverty levels since the Great Society was enacted, and even attributing that decrease to the Great Society programs is generous at best, given that natural economic oscillations throughout American history have resulted in similar changes in poverty levels.

---

[30] From *Making Economic Sense*. A free copy can be viewed through Google Books.
[31] Taken from U.S. Census Bureau data.

Proponents of the Act argue that the Act is constitutional because it affects interstate commerce; this argument falls apart, however, considering that by law all health insurance policies must only cover individuals residing in the states in which the policy is issued. Despite the fact that he Act is clearly unconstitutional, as it oversteps the federal government's authority significantly, it has been seen throughout this work that this is hardly a significant problem, given the history of the federal government's activity, and that the only check on federal power now seems to be a branch of the federal government itself, in the form of the Supreme Court. In the event that this law is determined to be constitutional, there is effectively nothing that the federal government cannot force an American citizen to buy, there being no qualitative difference, for example, between a health insurance policy and a bag of frozen broccoli.

In addition to the concerns attendant to compelling a citizen to purchase what amounts to a particular private-industry product, there is an additional problem associated with moving in the direction of a government-run health services industry (and make no mistake, such a system is the end-game of the minds behind the Affordable Care Act), and this particular problem not only concerns liberty, but in a very real way can amount to a matter of life or death. This problem currently manifests itself in numerous federal, local, and state programs which make health problems, and their associated personal behaviors, matters of public policy. In various locations across the country, localities have banned such things as kid's meal toys, soda vending machines, and salt shakers on restaurant tables. Some of the limitations, such as the ban many states have on smoking in restaurants and other public locations, even make things more enjoyable for the majority of Americans who do not smoke. What they also do, however, is place a limitation on the private property rights of restaurant and other service-industry business owners, as well as attempt to regulate what should be the private behavioral choices of American citizens. In every case where these regulatory schemes are implemented, the same argument is used: the regulations are for the public good, and promote public health. While individuals' personal behaviors are certainly no legitimate government concern (and in the case of the national government, off-limits constitutionally), there is a reason that government gets involved: in a very real way, as we move toward a single-payer system, a healthy lifestyle, or lack thereof, hits the national bottom line. Health care costs are already given as part of the justification for the public health reasoning behind compelling particular behavior, and as the government takes an increasing role overseeing the health services industry, such justifications are only going to increase. The ultimate conclusion to such a line of reasoning, of course, is that the government will begin to take costs into account when determining health care options. Proponents of a single payer system denigrate such claims, but such has been seen to be the case in nations where such systems exist, and these bottom-line decisions can often result in fatal consequences for those who live under such decisions. The problems with the Affordable Care Act, then, are threefold; first, such an act is clearly unconstitutional, given an understanding of the founders' intentions for the national government; second, such a system is antithetical to liberty, in that it promotes not only a limitation of choices in how individuals will exercise their option with regard to health care services; and third, it promotes a government system that reduces human worth to a quantifiable bottom-line value, rather than accepting that humans are intrinsically valuable.

## *Consequences of the Welfare State*

One thing that cannot be stressed enough is that the current welfare entitlement system in not sustainable: Social Security and Medicare/Medicaid are alone enough to bankrupt the national government, given current trends. In a very real sense, to argue for the continuance of these systems is to argue against reality itself; to claim that we face a choice between the entitlement state and the elimination of said state is to create a false dichotomy. The system as it currently exists will collapse; it is a matter of when and not if. Massive tax increases or additional reckless borrowing will kick the can down the road a few years, but not indefinitely, and both of these stop-gap measures will only make the final outcome worse.

In addition to economic disaster, these programs have been failures. Poverty rates are not significantly better than they were 50, 60, or even 70 years ago. While the Great Society and subsequent programs may make social activists feel better about "doing something," said something has been a dismal failure by any standard, and at the cost of trillions of dollars. That Americans have been subject to the confiscation of the fruits of their labor along with the sacrifice of individual liberty in order to prop up a failure of a system only makes the entire situation even more difficult to swallow. Were Americans to simply accept that private charities and private management of personal health care choices result in a cheaper, more effective system that preserves individual liberty, a looming financial disaster could be averted.

# Eight

# The Warfare State

*"In the councils of government, we must guard against the acquisition of unwarranted influence, whether sought or unsought, by the military-industrial complex. The potential for the disastrous rise of misplaced power exists and will persist."*
Dwight Eisenhower

One of the founding generation's greatest fears was the existence of a standing Army. Under both the Articles of Confederation and the Constitution, no provision was made for a permanent infantry force; instead, the states were expected to maintain a well-armed militia, which could be called up by the Congress in the event that the nation needed to go to war. The reasons for a distrust of a standing army were fairly simple: part of the conflict with the British that led to the Revolution had arisen because the troops that the British garrisoned in America's cities were seen as foreign occupiers, and the Colonists were required by law to board those troops. Additionally, many of the men tasked with forming the new nation recognized that a nation with a strong military would eventually feel compelled to use it, whether circumstances called for it or not. However, far from being anti-military, the framers did see the need for a defense force; In the Constitution, the writers recognized that in order to properly conduct foreign trade, as well as protect the shared national coastline borders, a United States Navy was required; the Navy to this day remains the only military branch specifically enumerated in the Constitution.

### The First World War and American Interventionism

While the United States' rise to military dominance is typically charted beginning with the Second World War, the part played by the Progressives, chiefly Woodrow Wilson, during the First World War cannot be overlooked. As has been stated earlier, the Progressive movement was characterized by a belief that the primary driver behind societal change should be the government, not individuals. It was during the reign of the Progressives that government grew at its most rapid pace; it should be no surprise, then, that the military would follow suit.

When war broke out in Europe in 1914, Americans at large were opposed to any United States involvement. Although there had been a number of small-scale military operations undertaken by the United States early in the century, they had been focused primarily in the Western hemisphere, and were largely limited to protecting U.S. interests in small Caribbean nations and through Central America. These nations historically have been politically unstable, and it was frequently necessary to protect embassies, consulates, and U.S. nationals conducting business in these nations during the frequent civil uprisings that occurred.

The culture of non-interventionism, however, did not stop corporate interests in the United States from profiting off of the war. In one example of this, Bethlehem Steel, helmed by industrialist Charles Schwab, contracted with the British government to supply several million artillery shells, along with ten submarines. This contract was in direct violation of U.S. law, which forbade military sales to foreign nations, but the Wilson administration, though it was aware of the deal, made no attempt to stop it.

Indeed, though publicly Wilson orated against the war and opposed American entry, even going so far as to base his 1916 re-election campaign on the slogan "He kept us out of war," it seemed that the White House was intent on eventually wading into the conflict. While this seems a serious charge, Wilson himself admitted that, were the United States on the winning side of the conflict, the sitting president would enjoy a much increased world status. In regards to the eventual peace process, Wilson opined that "as head of a nation participating in the war, the president of the United States would have a seat at the peace table, but... if he remained the representative of a neutral country, he could at best only 'call through a crack in the door.[32]'" As a man possessed of both great personal ambition and a desire to see the American government grow in prominence and power, the desire to see the United States' entry into this great conflict becomes clear.

Wilson had his wish; the Germans refused to cease submarine attacks against merchant shipping, and when a number of American vessels were sunk while in transit from the United States to Great Britain shortly after Wilson's second term began in 1917, he requested, and was

---

[32] This quote was spoken to 1931 Nobel Peace laureate Jane Addams, who later reported it to others.

granted, a declaration of war against Germany. During the year that the United States participated in the Great War, a half-million of America's young men were killed as a result of combat, and the United States would change its historical position of non-engagement to one of active participation in world conflicts. Ironically, Wilson's primary goal of entering the war; namely the expansion of the United States government's influence at home and abroad, would be a dismal failure. Britain and France were able to exert much more influence on the peace process than the United States, and the United States senate would reject American involvement in Wilson's brainchild, the League of Nations.

### *World War II and the Emergence of a Superpower*

The First World War had been referred to as the "War to end all wars." For some reason, the world consciousness was convinced that the massive toll in human life and property destruction would somehow lead to an era in which armed conflict was unthinkable. This, of course, was utter nonsense. In truth, while the United States would return to the Western Hemisphere and soon begin, as discussed earlier in this work, one of the most prosperous decades in its short history, Europe was left devastated and, amidst the licking of its collective wounds, the seeds of war would be sown once again.

In the Treaty of Versailles, which ended World War I, France and Great Britain sought to punish the Germans, upon whom they placed exclusive blame for the conflict. Germany lost all of its colonial holdings, and a significant amount of land within its own borders, primarily to France and Poland. In addition, Germany was required to pay reparations to its enemies, which amounted to approximately $442 billion in 2012 U.S. dollars. Between the loss of land and the payment of reparations, Germany was thoroughly devastated, and relied on loans from the United States to make many of the reparations payments. To get an idea of just how devastating the reparations payments were, the final payment was finally made in 2010[33] (although Adolf Hitler's rise to power was one reason for the delay in repayment).

As has been covered in numerous historical texts, bitterness over the Treaty of Versailles played no small part in Adolf Hitler's rise to power, and the total devastation in Europe (an entire generation of men had nearly been wiped out) led to an inability to produce the food, goods, and services needed to maintain the continent, and a severe depression, coinciding closely with the United States' own, broke out. The stage was therefore set for another European war, which broke out in 1938. In much the same way as had been done during the First World War, the United States officially stayed out of the conflict, having its own financial crisis to deal with, but supplies once again flowed freely to Great Britain.

In December of 1941, the United States, while considered a major player on the world stage by this time, was far from its current position as the single largest military force on the planet. While the U.S. had eventually entered the "War to end all wars" under President Woodrow Wilson's leadership, there had been something of a backlash against the interventionism undertaken during his presidency, and there had been little focus on expanding military capability during the period between the first and second World Wars. Coupled with this isolationist backlash, the nation had plunged into a deep depression during the last year of the 1920's, and

---

[33] Reported on *Time* magazine's website on October 4, 2010

extravagant military spending would not have been prudent, nor tolerated by the American people. This is not to imply that the United States was unprepared to fight a war, merely that militarism had not been the focus of American efforts during this period.

Therefore, when the Japanese navy attacked Pearl Harbor on December 7, 1941, many Americans were stunned. The United States had largely avoided involvement in the conflict that had enveloped Europe. They had begun supporting Great Britain materially, as had been the case during the First World War, and, more importantly for the Japanese, had begun an oil embargo against the island nation which threatened the military power of the small nation, who had begun efforts to conquer parts of the Asian mainland, including China and Siberia. It was this embargo, coupled with a general fear that the United States would eventually enter the war against Germany, a Japanese ally, which prompted the attack.

The American response had been immediate and hardly unjustified: a declaration of war against Japan was passed, and preparations were undertaken to retaliate against the surprise attack. Germany responded by declaring war against the United States, and America was, for the second time in less than half of a century, embroiled in a global conflict.

Unlike World War I, the Second World War was very technologically focused. Where the First World War was fought largely by infantry forces on foot and in trenches, the new conflict would take advantage of large armored tanks, fighter planes and bombers, and massive naval vessels, including the aircraft carrier, which had been developed near the end of the previous world conflict. This shift meant that an entire industry devoted to the development and manufacture of war machines could be supported, and it is in the Second World War that many of the United States' military equipment contractors, such as Northrop and Grumman, find their roots.

While the United States had briefly participated in the First World War, its participation in the Second was much larger, in duration as well as in scope. The American military managed to not only play the deciding role in the European theatre, but single-handedly defeated the Empire of Japan in the Pacific as well. Throughout the conflict, the United States focused on increasingly complex and devastating weapons, culminating in the detonation of the first atomic weapons in New Mexico and eventually Japan. The amount of time and effort spent in developing these weapons can hardly be over stated, and by the end of the war, the United States emerged as one of two nations whose military might dwarfed the rest of the globe. In a very real sense, the Second World War marked a very real shift in American military philosophy; while the United States had never shied from conflict, and indeed had a somewhat checkered past with regards to the way warfare had been used to acquire territory, it was at this point that the American military moved solidly toward a professional, rather than militia-style force, and it was also the point at which the military-industrial complex, that grey area where it is hard to tell where the government-led military ends and private-owned warfare industry begins, was born.

### *The Cold War*

Almost immediately following the conclusion of the Second World War, another conflict began, only this time it would be between two titans, with the rest of the globe merely as pawns. While the United States had clearly emerged as a superpower as the dust cleared in Berlin, they were not alone; the Soviet Union had marched across the eastern half of Germany, and while they had abruptly pulled out of the First World War due to a civil revolution, the resulting Communist state had proven itself a mighty military power. That the Soviet Union was both powerful, as well as Communist, which was at least ostensibly anathema to American ideals, led to immediate tensions between the two nations.

In terms of advancement of America's warfare state, the importance of the resulting conflict, which spanned more than four decades from the end of the Second World War in 1945 to the fall of the Soviet Union in 1991, cannot be overstated. Due in part to reconstruction, but then continued in order to maintain proximity to the Soviets, a large number of United States military installations were built in a number of European nations, from Iceland to Turkey, and thousands of United States military personnel are posted in these locations even today. In addition, weapons research and construction was continued in earnest, particularly in the area of nuclear weapons, with a peak stockpile of over 31,000 warheads built.

In addition to the perceived Soviet threat, China became a Communist nation in 1949, and fears of the spread of Communism throughout Asia were used to justify military incursions into both Korea and Vietnam during the 1950's, 1960' and 1970's. While these two military actions are well known, it is less well known that, during the same period, and continuing through the 1980's, the United States military conducted smaller operations in Lebanon, Congo, Thailand, Cambodia, Laos, Egypt, Grenada, Honduras, Cuba, and the Dominican Republic. It is important to note that these operations, including the larger conflicts in Korea and Vietnam, were not in response to direct threats against United States citizens. This is a marked departure from military action prior to the Second World War, when less frequent (although still numerous) military deployments had occurred primarily to directly protect U.S. citizens in areas that had become dangerous due to local unrest. Instead, in these cases, the express purpose of committing American troops and equipment to armed conflict was to stop the spread of Communism, which, while not seen as a direct threat to United States citizens or territory, was nonetheless seen as in the United States' strategic interest.

The cold war posed a serious threat to civil liberties within the borders of the United States as well. Just as American military power was brought to bear against supporters of Communism across the globe, an increasingly powerful police state was being built to fight Communist threats at home. This is not to say that no threat existed; during the period following the Second World War, the Communist philosophy, which is antithetical to the pursuits of a liberty-loving people, had indeed gained a foothold within the United States, particularly within the academy and arts communities. In fact, the House Committee on Un-American Activities (HUAC), which, along with its Senate counterpart, the Senate Committee on Government Operations, is often upheld as the case study for U.S. government violations of individual rights during this period, was supported in its early stages by such libertarian heroes as Ayn Rand, the founder of the Objectivist philosophy and author of the anti-government novel *Atlas Shrugged*. In 1947, Rand, a refugee who had fled to the United States from the Soviet Union in 1926, testified as a friendly witness to HUAC in an attempt to highlight pro-Communist propaganda being produced in Hollywood[34].

The real threat to civil liberties, as is typically the case, was occurring behind the scenes. In 1949, the National Security Resources Board (NSRB), which had been founded the same year Rand gave testimony to HUAC, put in place contingency plans to censor communications and limit press freedoms when and if it was deemed in the interests of national security to do so. Proponents of these plans claimed that such actions may become necessary during wartime, but the guidelines produced did not require a declaration of war, merely a declaration of a state of emergency from the President. At this point it should be noted that when the First Amendment was ratified during President Washington's first term, it was developed specifically to protect politically inconvenient speech; or speech during times of national emergency. That such is the case should be self-evident; for unless such pressures exist which would cause government to limit speech or press, none would be necessary. In other words, if the First Amendment only applies during peacetime, when speech and press freedoms are convenient, and therefore unlikely to encounter opposition, why have an amendment protecting them at all?

In addition to the NSRB's censorship plans, in 1950 the Federal Bureau of Investigation, under the leadership of J. Edgar Hoover, began compiling a database of individuals suspected of participating in "suspicious activities" which may indicate that they are potential threats to government authority. In the event of a national emergency, the nature of which remained conveniently undefined, the database could be used to round up suspicious persons for incarceration in internment camps run by the U.S. military. The illegality of such action has

---

[34] A transcript of this testimony is available at:
http://www.noblesoul.com/orc/texts/huac.html

previously been covered in discussions related to the internment of Japanese-Americans during the Second World War; it shall only be reiterated that the database activity likely violated the Fourth Amendment, and any internment activity would violate the due process clause of the Fifth Amendment, as well as the Jury Trial requirement of the Sixth Amendment.

Americans' Fourth Amendment rights against unlawful search and seizure were also violated over several decades, and under multiple operations, when their communications were monitored without warrant. During Operation Shamrock, an NSA operation which ran from 1945 to 1975, international communications originating in the United States, including those originating from United States citizens, were monitored for potentially subversive content. In 1967, a similar program, code-named MINARET, began, and ran concurrently with Shamrock under the supervision of the CIA and FBI. Both operations were terminated in 1975 when the Church Committee, which had been convened to study intelligence gathering in the wake of the Watergate affair, uncovered their operational plans and made clear their intention to initiate criminal investigations against members of the agencies for Fourth Amendment violations.

### *Korea and the War Powers Act*

As has previously been highlighted, Article I, Section 8 of the United States Constitution grants sole power for declaring war to the United States Congress. It is only with a declaration of war that the President is allowed to fully exercise his enumerated power as Commander In Chief of the armed forces. That such is the case is beyond question; Presidents Jefferson and Madison had explicitly made statements that they understood the Constitutional war-making power to lie solely in the Congress, and that they were powerless, even in the face of incitement from a foreign power, to send troops into war without a Congressional declaration. According to James Madison, "Those who are to conduct a war cannot, in the nature of things, be proper or safe judges whether a war ought to be commenced, continued, or concluded. They are barred from the latter functions by a great principle in free government, analogous to that which separates the sword from the purse, or the power from executing from the power of enacting laws.[35]" Even their contemporary, Alexander Hamilton, who had a vision of a much more powerful president, erred on the side of caution when it came to war. Hamilton referred, in *Federalist 69*, to the Presidential war power as that of "nothing more than ... first General and Admiral," indicating that while it was the president who would execute the war, power to initiate war lay with another. Subsequent presidents had all clearly understood that this was the case; in spite of their numerous flaws, even presidents Wilson and Roosevelt, hardly men to let the Constitution get in their way, requested declarations of war prior to entering hostilities in World Wars I and II, respectively (the exception to this being the U.S. Civil War, which was never declared because the Union viewed the Confederacy as an insurrection, rather than a war with a foreign sovereign nation).

Such would not be the case with Roosevelt's successor, Harry S. Truman. In 1950, completely counter to the actions of every one of his predecessors, Truman sent troops into combat in Korea without Congressional approval. His defense for such a blatantly unconstitutional action was that since military action was authorized by a United Nations resolution, he had authority to commit

---

[35] This statement was made during the Pacificus-Helvidius debates.

troops. There are several problems with this justification; first, the Constitution provides no such clause which places international treaties superior to Constitutional authority, and second, the United Nations charter itself contained no requirement for signatories to provide military support contingent on nothing more than a U.N. resolution. Clearly, Truman was well beyond his Constitutional authority, and in an earlier time, before the Constitution had been thoroughly stripped of power, would have been subject to impeachment and subsequent removal from office. However, no such action would come. Following an investigation into the event, author Charlie Savage wrote in 2007 that the reason Congress never held Truman to account for his actions was that Congressional members were desperate to appear tough on Communism, and feared that any action which did not show a solid front against this existential threat would make them appear weak.

In 1973, following the Vietnam conflict, which had been supported by Congressional resolution, Congress would, much as they had done during the Progressive era, cede yet more of their authority to the Executive branch. The result was the War Powers Resolution, which authorized the President to commit U.S. troops to combat, provided that he inform Congress within 48 hours of such activity, and provided that he obtain Congressional authorization for any conflict within 60 days of the commencement of hostilities, or cease operation. As with the advent of Executive rule making power at the beginning of the 20th Century, such abandonment of legislative authority is of dubious legality, since the Constitution does not provide a mechanism for Congress to cede its authority to the President, and such an action, as evidenced by Madison's comments highlighted above, clearly violate the spirit in which the writers of the Constitution viewed the delegation of powers. Nevertheless, the War Powers Resolution has been upheld by the courts, and the outcome has been an expansion in the use of United States military force in global conflicts not directly related to an imminent threat against the United States homeland; in fact, following the War Powers Resolution, there has not been a single war declared by the United States Congress, and there have been only four occasions in which a Congressional use of force declaration has been passed: forces were sent to Lebanon in 1983 as part of a force overseeing the withdrawal of the Palestine Liberation Organization (PLO), Operation Desert Storm in 1991, Operation Enduring Freedom in Afghanistan, beginning in 2001, and Operation Iraqi Freedom, which lasted from 2003 to 2011. In contrast, troops have been committed to combat operations without a declaration of war or Congressional approval in at least seven conflicts since the War Powers Resolution was passed, in Bosnia, Liberia, Haiti, Grenada, Somalia, Yugoslavia, and most recently in Libya. While the War Powers Resolution has been followed in most of these occasions, in at least two conflicts, in Yugoslavia and Libya, hostilities lasted longer than 60 days with no Congressional approval. In both cases, the defense raised by the President has been that, as in the case with the Korean conflict, action was undertaken in accordance with United Nations resolutions. This, of course, raises a number of problems. First, the action is illegal, according to both the War Powers Resolution and the Constitution, and appealing to an authority outside of the United States does not change this fact. To act in defiance of the law when your job description specifically entails that you uphold United States law, as the President's description does, is not only immoral and unethical, but damages the very fabric of society. Second, one of the greatest threats to liberty through the history of this nation has been the sequestering of power away from the populace and into the executive branch. Further removing that power by moving it into an international body, which is in no way accountable to anyone in the American public is to throw away the idea of self-governance upon which the United States was founded.

### *September 11, 2001 and Its Aftermath*

Throughout the course of this work, there have been two things that have allowed the federal government to seize and centralize power: economics and war. Financial crises have been used to seize control of the nation's economy, and military crises have been used to curtail individual liberty. In post-New Deal America, nowhere has the second abuse been more on display than the government's actions in response to the September 11, 2001 attacks on the World Trade Center and the Pentagon.

In the aftermath of the attacks, President George Bush proposed a reorganization of the nation's security apparatus. This reorganization would include the establishment of yet another cabinet-level department, which became known as the Department of Homeland Security. A number of agencies that were previously in existence, including U.S. Customs and Border Protection, the United States Coast Guard, the United States Secret Service, and the Federal Emergency Management Agency, were moved to the new department. In addition, a new federal agency, the Transportation Security Administration (TSA), was created to oversee airport security nationwide.

It is the newest agency on this list, the Transportation Security Administration, which has come under the most scrutiny for its violations of individual liberties. One of the chief concerns among civil libertarians is that it is now required to undergo a search of your person by a federal agent before boarding an aircraft. The airline, which is a private business, has no say in the matter, nor does the passenger. This seems to be a clear violation of the Fifth Amendment, which requires probable cause and a warrant before a citizen can be subjected to a search of their persons or effects. Proponents of the security measures argue that such actions are necessary in order to prevent further use of commercial aircraft as weapons against U.S. targets, but this argument has two key flaws: first, the measures are illegal, and the fact that they are permitted is another assault on the rule of law in the United States. Second, there have been two known incidents of individuals smuggling explosives onboard commercial airliners since the Transportation Security Administration took over airport security in the United States. In one of the incidents, Umar Farouk Abdulmutallab boarded a Detroit-bound aircraft from Amsterdam with plastic explosives hidden in his underwear, and in the other, Richard Ried passed through a Paris checkpoint and boarded a Miami-bound flight with plastic explosives in his shoe. On the domestic front, there have been cases, such as that of Faisal Shahzad, a suspected terrorist who passed through a TSA checkpoint at JFK airport in New York, although he was on a federal watch list. These three incidents showcase different problems with the TSA model: in the first two, the system was merely ineffective, demonstrating that flights originating from foreign soil represent a significant hole in defenses; the third, however, has shown that even with nearly a quarter of a million employees and a $55 billion annual budget, the federal government cannot keep known terrorists or explosives off of commercial aircraft, even when they are allowed to violate citizens' Fifth Amendment rights. Whether ineffective or incompetent, it is clear that the current system does not work.

Not all security related rights violations have been perpetrated by the Department of Homeland Security. In December 2005, the *New York Times* reported on a National Security Agency (NSA) surveillance program that resulted in the monitoring and recording of thousands of communications between American citizens and foreigners. The NSA argued that, under the Foreign Intelligence Surveillance Act (FISA), the NSA had the authority to monitor the communications of any foreign person, regardless of whether the individual on the other end of the line was an American citizen or not. It has also since been revealed by telecommunications experts that it can be nearly impossible to determine the exact location of an individual involved in a cell phone call or e-mail exchange, and that as a result, the NSA program may very well involve the monitoring of communications between two individuals inside the United States, in violation of both FISA requirements and the Fifth Amendment. It should also be noted that this program is virtually indistinguishable from Operations Shamrock and MINARET, which were undertaken during the Cold War, both of which were shut down in the face of Congressional and public pressure, as both were seen as obvious violations of Constitutional rights.

On the purely domestic front, the Federal Bureau of Investigation was given broad discretion post-9/11 to collect records related to individuals suspected of terrorist activities. At the center of the controversy is a document known as a national security letter, a form of administrative subpoena that can be issued by any supervisory-level Special Agent and requires the release of documentation that previously required a warrant issued by a judge. Once again, this represents an unconstitutional shift of power from the Judicial to the Executive branch, in clear violation of the Fifth Amendment. Not only is this activity unconstitutional and at odds with the idea of individual liberty, but it has been abused beyond even its original intent: an internal Department of Justice audit released in 2007 showed that the FBI used these powers illegally to obtain records on American citizens.

The response to these criticisms, which has been more or less the same response to all challenges to the broad police powers enacted in response to the threat of terrorism, is that the measures are necessary in order to ensure Americans' security. Like the internment of Japanese-Americans in World War II, or the prosecution of war dissenters in World War I, it seems that the government will never tire of using the specter of war to limit personal liberty.

### *The Warfare State and the Founders*

As previously stated, this work has the primary purpose of detailing the many deviations from founding ideals that this nation has chosen, and to demonstrate how such deviations have resulted in a nation that is, in general, less free than its founders intended, and, in fact, resembles in many ways the empire that they fought to separate from. While this entire work attempts to fulfill this purpose, the discussion of the militaristic aspects of the United States' history, perhaps more than any other, provides a microcosm within which to view the entire progression.

What many individuals may not realize is that the founders were suspicious of military power to such a degree that they did not even support the idea of a standing army. Instead, they envisioned a nation where every individual made up part of the defensive force. Such an idea is not beyond comprehension; it was, of course, everyday citizens united in the cause of liberty who had defeated the professional British army during the Revolutionary War. The Second Amendment, in mentioning the militia, provides evidence for this ideal as well. The founders believed that a well-armed populace would be able to provide for their own defense and that as a result, a professional army would be unnecessary.

The desire to avoid a standing army is understandable; one of the complaints in the Declaration of Independence was that colonists were forced to quarter troops, and were subjected to the presence of a standing army. In considering the founders' position, there are three primary arguments against a standing army: first, having a professional military force at one's disposal increases the temptation to use it. Today's United States is an excellent example of this. If the entire force necessary for the invasions of Afghanistan, Iraq, and military operations in Libya were called up from reserve units (meaning men and women with day jobs), would the logistical effort and required preparation time, not to mention the disruption in domestic commerce, have been enough to keep these invasions from happening? Second, a standing army is expensive. Since the end of the Second World War, the military-industrial complex has grown to the point where close to a trillion dollars is spent annually keeping it going. There are a huge number of Americans who make their living from war and rumor of war. How much good could be accomplished if that money were allowed to remain in the private sector with free-market economics driving its use? Third, a standing army insulates the public at large from the horrors of war. Given the size and scope of the United States' military machine, it is unlikely that any conflict except a direct invasion of the homeland would cause the average American discomfort. Would Americans be less likely to support military conflict if they felt the results through austerity and a requirement of service? All of these questions resonated with the founders, who saw military action as something to be undertaken only as a last resort, not as a first option to be taken in foreign lands, merely for something as nebulous as national interest.

Over-regulation and high taxation are evil, and both contribute to the continuous assault on liberty that has occurred during the United States' history, but it may very well be our preoccupation with military might and national security which represents the greatest threat. Economic crisis and war have been used repeatedly and effectively to usurp personal liberty; indeed, there may be no personal freedom that Americans today will not cede if it is done so in the name of security, so afraid are we of Communists, Islamists, and other faceless enemies. This is not to say that Communism and Islamism do not represent threats; indeed they do. However, in both cases, the threat is that of authoritarianism. In one case, we submit to the power of the collective good; in the other we submit to Sharia and Allah's will. However, if we acquiesce to domestic authoritarianism in order to protect us from foreign authoritarianism, what have we gained? In order for our fight for liberty to succeed, liberty itself must be preserved. It is proper, then, in concluding the discussion of this great threat to liberty, to move on to what may be done to take the lessons of the last two hundred years and move into an age where freedom and liberty take precedence     in     our     collective     consciousness.

# Nine

# A Way Forward

*"The God who gave us life, gave us liberty at the same time."*
Thomas Jefferson

Modern political conservatives frequently idealize the past when outlining their political platform. The name 'conservative' implies that there is some point in the past where the proper ideals were in place, and the desire is to conserve the structure of that period. However, what time in America's history would be good to return to? Throughout the course of this work, it has been demonstrated that the entirety of American history has been a progression from liberty to authoritarianism; the implication in that statement being that the appropriate time period to return to would be before 1789, before there was a federal government to consolidate power, when the states were independent bodies and a free-market political and economic system was at its most pure. Indeed, there is much to admire about the principles upon which the

United States was founded, and in the Declaration of Independence we see some of the greatest statements related to Natural Law and the intrinsic value of man ever encapsulated within a government document.

However, when one looks at the reality of the situation in 1789, there are aspects which are wholly incompatible with a society that truly values freedom and individual liberty. Slavery, of course, is the prime example of reality not matching the ideal. The mere idea that one man can own another, and based solely on the color of his skin, is a violation of everything that the United States was founded on. There are other examples of this; the fact that women were denied both the right to own property and the right to vote, and the fact that native inhabitants of the country were forced off of land that they had occupied for generations should all give pause. Bringing these issues up, however, is not intended to be an indictment of the nation's founding principles; it is merely intended to highlight the fact that there is no particular time in American history to which it would be ideal to return.

Instead, it is far preferable to take the ideals upon which the United States was founded, namely liberty, freedom, and the recognition of private property, and attempt to apply them uniformly. It is also important to understand what has gone wrong over the past two centuries so that it can be prevented in the future. What is being proposed here, then, is not a return to 1789, but a look to the future, and a nation truly built upon the ideals of freedom and liberty.

### *Every Man A Criminal – The Code of Federal Regulations*

The specific historical events mentioned in this work demonstrate many of the events used to justify massive expansions of power for the national government, but these only account for a small fraction of the massive regulatory apparatus that has been built in Washington. Federal guidelines control the composition of gasoline, as well as the fuel efficiency for the vehicle that gasoline powers. Federal regulations limit the number of electronic transfers that can be made to and from a personal savings account (it's 6 per month, if you are curious) as well as the amount of cash you can withdraw from your personal account without notifying the federal government ($10,000). In 2007, Congress passed a law mandating that incandescent light bulbs be phased out over the following seven years, in order to increase the nation's energy efficiency. During the disastrous oil spill caused by British Petroleum's Deep Water Horizon offshore drilling platform in 2010, the U.S. Coast guard decided that volunteer cleanup boats would have to be docked until the proper federally-mandated safety inspections could be completed. All together, the entire Code of Federal Regulations is 152,246 pages long. The entire thing (all 229 volumes) can be ordered from the Government Printing Office for a total of $10,841.

In order to enforce all of these regulations, the federal government now employs over 4.4 million people, of which 2.8 million staff the executive-branch bureaucracies. All told, 1.4% of all Americans work for the federal government in some capacity. Federal employment in 1789 was approximately 3,000 out of a nation of 3.9 million, or 0.07%, meaning federal employment has grown as a percentage of the population by 20 times. It is not, however, just the number of people conducting the business of governing at the federal level that is of concern, but the scope of their authority. When George Washington took office in 1789, there were four cabinet-level offices:

War, State, Treasury, and Attorney General. Today, there are fifteen, most of which deal with areas not enumerated to the federal government in the Constitution, including Labor, Transportation, Health and Human Services, Energy, Education, Agriculture, and Housing and Urban Development. None of these agencies have missions dealing with a Constitutionally-enumerated power, but all claim regulatory authority over the aspects of American's lives that they oversee; aspects which, according to the tenth amendment, should be overseen either by the state in which a citizen resides, or by the individual.

In order to comply with the litany of regulations, many companies have to employ a full time staff of regulatory compliance specialists, whose sole duty is to make sure that the company is following all of the thousands of pages of regulations relevant to the company's operation. These labor costs are nothing but a waste, since those specialists contribute nothing to the company's productivity. Furthermore, many of these regulations make the corporations that they affect less efficient, thereby reducing their competitiveness with foreign competitors who do not have the same burdensome regulations.

These problems, however, are not the biggest threat that the regulatory apparatus represents. As mentioned, the current federal regulatory code is over 150,000 pages long. Were any individual to read the code at a rate of 100 pages/day (an aggressive pace, considering the legislative language used), it would take them over four years to complete the task. Since most people have to work for a living at something other than reading federal code, it means that the average American has absolutely no idea what the law really is, and likely violates it on a regular basis. This, of course, is part of government's goal; it wants to make every man a criminal so that it can selectively prosecute individuals in order to coerce a particular type of behavior. This is the antithesis of liberty, and something that author Ayn Rand warns against in her novel *Atlas Shrugged:*

> "The only power any government has is the power to crack down on criminals. Well, when there aren't enough criminals, one makes them. One declares so many things to be a crime that it becomes impossible for men to live without breaking laws."

### *At the Crossroads*

As America enters the second decade of the twenty-first century, the challenges it faces are numerous. The current regulatory environment has set up massive corporations who conspire with the federal government to make it increasingly difficult for small business to succeed. The regulatory environment, while itself unconstitutional, also results in a marketplace that is less free, and as a result, gives fewer choices to the American public at a higher cost. While the Progressive movement in the early 20th Century claimed to desire an end to monopolization, the true effect of their policies was to make it less possible for upstarts to challenge the big businesses that have made peace with their federal masters.

On the political front, there is also far less choice than there was when the nation was founded. With a strong emphasis on state's rights, the United States was founded in a free political market, as well as a free economic market. One of the great things about America was that there was free trade and free passage among a group of semi-autonomous states, which resulted in competition between those states for residents. Over the past two centuries, more and more power has been ceded to the federal government, resulting in fewer and fewer meaningful differences between the states. Today, the differences between living and working in Oklahoma or North Carolina may seem significant, but they are far less so when viewed through the lens of the freedom those states should experience.

As a result of the security apparatus, American citizens are subjected to searches of their person and effects that would never have been allowed in the eighteenth century. The extent to which Americans are monitored in the name of safety or national security is staggering, coming from a government founded by men who believed that the only rightful function of government was the preservation of private property rights. In many cases, Americans have given up their rights in the name of preserving them.

The American people have, in many cases, been bought and paid for in order to continue this power grab. Nearly half of all Americans receive some form of federal financial assistance, and according to 2009 federal tax returns, 46% of Americans pay no federal income tax at all. The fact that almost half of the nation relies at least somewhat on federal funding for sustenance, while the number of individuals paying for these programs shrinks every year, shows the difficulty reformers will have in convincing the American public that real changes need to be made.

The results of the slide from federal republic to authoritarian state are staggering. As of the fourth quarter of 2011, the United States is more than $15 trillion in debt, with over $100 trillion in unfunded mandates, thanks primarily to Medicare and Social Security obligations. The out of control federal debt, combined with an unwillingness to address the root causes, has resulted in a downgrade of United States credit from AAA to AA+, indicating that investors no longer see U.S. bonds as the safe investment they used to be. In fact, economists are now looking into the future and seeing a potential U.S. bankruptcy, an event that would be catastrophic not only to Americans but to the rest of the world as well.

The debt and regulation have also affected the way U.S. freedom is perceived. The Heritage Foundation, a U.S.-based research institution, each year compiles a list of the freest economies in the world. It would be expected that the United States, founded in the principles of freedom and liberty espoused by men such as John Locke and Adam Smith, would receive top marks. However, in 2012, the Heritage Foundation rated the United States number 10 on its list, following nations such as Australia, Switzerland, Ireland, and Canada. This is a drop from the previous year, when it was ranked 9, itself a drop from 2010, when it was ranked 8. It appears that not only is the United States lagging in economic freedom; it is becoming less free each year.

It is very clear that the United States is in trouble. However, it also is apparent that the problems plaguing the nation are easily identifiable. In fact, as the nation has slid farther and farther from the representative republic to a socialist democracy, many of the problems the nation faces, even those that additional government effort has been put into to solve, have gotten worse. Therefore, the United States faces a choice: continue down the current path, which results in a populace enslaved to its federal masters and an inevitable bankruptcy, or take a new path, one that retains the best of the founding principles while improving on the ideas of liberty and freedom upon which this nation was built.

### *Lessons Learned*

As the Constitutional Convention wrapped up in 1787, Benjamin Franklin was approached by a woman who wanted to know what kind of government the delegates had designed for the young nation. "A republic, if you can keep it," was Franklin's reply. In those seven words, Franklin revealed much of the wisdom for which he was so famous. In this statement, he managed to encapsulate the entire problem with the Constitutional endeavor: the republic would have to be maintained, or like so many other governments throughout the ages, it would descend into tyranny and oppression. Indeed, many of the delegates themselves had serious concerns about the government they had committed to paper; there was a fear that the new federal government would become too powerful and consume the states that it was intended to serve. Many in that crowded Philadelphia hall only hesitatingly approved of the idea of a president, because they saw in the presidency the specter of a kingship; the very thing many of them had fought against on the battlefields of the Revolutionary War.

Thomas Jefferson, no fan of the Constitution, once opined that "The natural progress of things is for liberty to yield and government to gain ground." Jefferson was extremely concerned about the centralization of power allowed by the Constitution, and foresaw the steady slide from liberty to tyranny that would occur over the following two centuries.

Echoing the concerns of Franklin and Jefferson in a speech to the Phoenix Chamber of Commerce in 1961, future president Ronald Reagan made the following observation:

"Freedom is never more than one generation away from extinction. We didn't pass it to our children in the bloodstream. It must be fought for, protected, and handed on for them to do the same, or one day we will spend our sunset years telling our children and our children's children what it was once like in the United States where men were free."

With all due respect to Reagan, his warning came too late. By the time 1961 rolled around, the damage had been done. If any lesson can be taken from the Constitution, it is this: the centralization of power was a mistake, and even the best of intentions can be exploited by those who thirst for power. While men like Franklin devoted their lives to liberty, it was their misplaced faith that others would do the same that has doomed the United States to a future "telling our children and our children's children what it was once like in the United States where men were free."

### *A Modest Proposal*

If, however, we truly believe that freedom is the greatest moral good that a government can provide for its people, there is a way to a brighter future, and while not easy, the path is simple. Below are outlined the keys to returning our nation to one where liberty, freedom, and the rights of the individual reign supreme. The way forward must make a path through the following principles:

*Recognition that all men are created equal.* In George Orwell's *Animal Farm*, the animals overthrow the tyranny of the farmer in an attempt to rule themselves. It is not long, however, before the pigs are able to set themselves up as the new rulers, and the statement that "All animals are equal" becomes "All animals are equal, but some are more equal than others." In the United States, corporatism, political patronage, identity politics, and blind greed have created a situation where there are two groups: the political elite and everyone else. Recognition that all humans are intrinsically equal in value, and that no man should rule over another, is the foundational building block upon which liberty must be built. The fact that there was a blatant violation of this principle in the early days of the republic has been used repeatedly, and effectively, by those wishing to discredit the ideas of the nation's founders. The irony in this is that they are using the intellectual inconsistency of the founders to bring an end to the good ideas, not the poor behavior. Those wishing to abandon liberty are attempting to sell their fellow countrymen into slavery. There is no middle ground.

*Recognition that all men are created equal, but not entitled to equal outcome.* Another way to put this is that 'liberty results in inequality.' There is a large measure of responsibility involved in living in a society where the government doesn't steal from the productive to give to the unproductive. Therefore, a political system focused on liberty results in inequality. This comes from the fact that people have different levels of skill, intelligence, and drive. As a result, some will work harder than others, some will innovate more than others, and some will produce a product that is superior to others. In a free market, we would expect that the 'best and brightest' will end up at the top of the financial hierarchy, while those with less skill, drive, or intellect will end up at the bottom. The fact is that not everyone can win in a free market, despite what some free-market proponents say. To argue that this is not true in a free society is silly. However, it is actually the best possible system, even given the fact that it produces economic winners and losers.

First, let's take a look at the fundamental assertion that a society with winners and losers is a bad thing. This pervasive idea has its roots in the second industrial revolution, when families like the Vanderbilts and Rockefellers made gigantic fortunes over the course of a few decades. Progressive politicians like Teddy Roosevelt and Woodrow Wilson used these families in order to foment class warfare and gain political power, and the ideas that they put in the heads of the American electorate persist to this day. However, what we should realize is that the same conditions that made these families unbelievably wealthy also allowed the average American family to achieve a standard of living unheard of only a few years earlier. In this situation, the old adage that 'a rising tide lifts all boats' certainly holds true. In a free-market society, even the losers enjoy the advantages of a wealthy society, which leads into the second point: *there is no pie.*

Politicians who use class warfare to gain power have convinced a large segment of the public that if someone wins, it is at everyone else's expense. This is, of course, false. While there are corrupt people (in both politics and business) who will take advantage of others in order to gain for themselves, this is not the only way, or even the most common way, that people become wealthy. Typically, the wealthy get where they are through a combination of hard work, intellect, skill, and luck. And while there are some poor souls out there who have ended up at the bottom due to the unethical actions of others or bad luck, the vast majority are there because of bad decisions, lack of drive, skill, intelligence, or some combination thereof. The important thing to note here is that wealth is not a zero-sum game; just because someone becomes a millionaire, it does not condemn another to a life in the poor house.

Third, it is important to understand that liberty and equality are mutually exclusive, if what we mean by equality is actually 'equality of outcome.' In order to guarantee equality of outcome, which is the goal of socialist societies, it is necessary to take from one and give to another. This is embodied in the central doctrine of Marxism, "from each according to his ability, to each according to his need." When the fruits of one man's labor are subject to the enjoyment of another, this is the definition of servitude, which is the antithesis of liberty. This cannot be stressed enough: *liberty and forced equality (socialism) cannot coexist, as they are by definition opposites.* Therefore, you have to choose between liberty and equality of outcome.

Fourth, history shows us that all political systems have winners and losers. If you believe that authoritarian socialist systems produce equality, you are mistaken. Historically, these systems have produced two classes of people: the political elite and everyone else. These systems rely on nepotism and political connections, rather than intellect, drive, and skill in order to choose their winners and losers, which actually makes them *less* fair than libertarian systems.

Americans have, by and large, bought into a Progressive lie that "all men are created equal" means that "all men are guaranteed an equal outcome." They have also bought into the lie that true liberty and false 'equality' can coexist. We need to recognize that these are lies, and decide if we want to be a society that embraces liberty, or one that robs from the rich to give to the poor.

*Recognition that all men are entitled to life, liberty, and property.* John Locke's original statement was modified by

Thomas Jefferson in the final draft of the Declaration of Independence to read "life, liberty, and the pursuit of happiness" because it was feared that the word 'property' would give the impression that slavery was being codified in the nation's founding principles. The founders knew that slavery was wrong, but were unable or unwilling to do anything about it, resulting in a weakening of the statement supporting private property. The biggest problem here is that, excepting the ownership of humans, the recognition of private property is the second most important key to liberty. That which a man owns is his to do with as he sees fit; if a man owns nothing, then he has no rights, because wherever he lives, works, or travels, he does so on someone else's property. In nations where there is no private property, everything belongs either to the government, in which case its ownership is limited to the few in power, or to the mob, in which case its ownership lies with whoever has the ability to rule it by force.

*Recognition that all men are entitled to is life, liberty, and the pursuit of property.* This statement is only a slight modification to the statement above, but it makes a large point: no one is entitled to anything other than their life, their liberty, and the property that they acquire as a result of their work. This is a direct challenge to Progressives who want to use the power of the state to implement wealth redistribution under the guise of human rights. To say that something is a 'human right' is to say that every human is entitled to it. The classical liberal view of rights, as outlined by thinkers such as John Locke, and enshrined in the American enterprise by Thomas Jefferson, is that human rights are freedoms that every human should enjoy. One of those freedoms is freedom from compulsion, meaning that you cannot be forced to do something for someone else.

However, modern liberalism has completely redefined the term 'human rights' to mean that there are things, rather than freedoms, that all humans are entitled to. To say that someone has a 'right' to a thing like health care, for example, means that someone must be *forced* to provide it; either the doctor will be forced to treat at gunpoint, or someone will have his wages taken at gunpoint to pay the doctor. Either way results in forced labor. This, then, is the heart of true freedom: *My rights cannot come as the result of the servitude of another.*

*Recognition that governments exist solely to protect life and private property rights.* In *Common Sense*, Thomas Paine argues that if man was righteous, governments would be unnecessary. It is because man tends to cheat, steal, and murder, that individuals create governments. The purpose of governments is specifically to prevent the kind of behavior that violates the rights of another. Anything beyond the preservation of life and private property is an illegitimate exercise of power, because it robs individuals of their liberty. During the 20th Century, the federal government's powers were expanded to regulate private labor in the form of minimum wage and overtime laws, along with regulatory support for union organization. Since these regulations insert government into matters of private association, and regulate the rights of property owners, they are illegitimate uses of government power. Labor, like agricultural products or oil, is a commodity, and the price for a man's labor should be determined by the market and the man's willingness to work for a particular wage. Additionally, minimum wage and overtime laws contribute to youth unemployment and price inflation, meaning that there are fewer people working, and those that are working are paying higher prices on goods and services in order to cover the price of artificially high wages. The economic effect resulting from such government involvement is a net negative.

In addition to regulating private association, Americans have decided that government should provide for the poor. Since government has no money of its own, the only way to accomplish this task is to take money from those that produce wealth and give it to those who do not. While this stance may sound cold, and is demonized in the political sphere as uncaring, the fact is that wealth redistribution violates the federal government's primary directive to protect private property. There is nothing that forbids the states from caring from the poor (as many did prior to the current entitlement scheme), and Americans should, as a matter of personal morality, give to charitable institutions that support the needy. It is not, however, within the purview of a properly functioning federal body, and, constitutional considerations aside, if private charity deals with the problem of poverty more thoroughly and efficiently than government, it is only prudent for state and local governments to follow the same path.

*Recognition that liberty requires responsibility.* The idea of freedom is very popular. From a young age, Americans learn to appeal to the liberties that have been enshrined in the Bill of Rights, such as freedom of speech and expression. There is, however, a catch. In most of those appeals to liberty, the focus is on what liberty gives us - things like the ability to say what we want, or wear the clothes we want, or practice the religion that we want (or even none at all). Yet what many fail to recognize is that true liberty means that there is no safety net. If someone falls, they must rely on family, friends, and community for support, instead of an intrusive government. It means that if someone cannot feed their family, they must ask for help from people they know, instead of hiding behind a faceless bureaucracy. It also means that those who have more than they need must give freely, and without compulsion, to those truly in need. Liberty requires responsibility. It means that we are ultimately responsible for ourselves.

The concepts above are not complex; they can be understood by nearly anyone. What they are, however, is controversial. Americans have become accustomed to the illusion of security that the current situation provides. There is an ample safety net, such that it is inconceivable that even if unemployed and left with no income, any American would go without a television, cell phone, or a car, unless it is by choice. The problem with this situation is twofold, however. First, the only way for government to provide this kind of security is for Americans to lose their liberty. Second, the current situation is insolvent; the government borrows a quarter of what it spends, with no solution to the deficit crisis in sight. Eventually, the system will come crashing down; the only choice we have is whether to fix it or allow it to collapse and attempt to pick up the pieces.

### *Toward a More Perfect Union*

What is needed now is something similar to the Constitutional Convention of 1787. The United States government is broken, and it needs to be fixed. In this situation, though, the federal government does not suffer from being too weak, but too overbearing. The reforms that need to be put in place, with an eye to the principles outlined above, must be specific in nature, since the federal government has become an expert at using ambiguity to expand its powers. The following are a list of changes that would result in an expansion of liberty for every American:

*Enforce the 10th Amendment.* According to the Bill of Rights, "The powers not delegated to the United States by the Constitution, nor prohibited by it to the States, are reserved to the States respectively, or to the people." According to the original text of the Constitution, the powers delegated by the Constitution are fairly specific and limited in scope. The reason for this can be summed up in a single word: decentralization. The founders believed that with powers vested primarily in the states, but with those states bound together in a single nation that promised free passage and a common currency and language, the states would be forced to compete with each other for the best citizens. In effect, the 10th Amendment was intended to create a kind of market competition amongst the states. A state which implemented burdensome taxation or regulatory schemes would have to compete for business and labor resources with a state that was friendlier to commercial interests. Likewise, the state with a heavy tax burden may offer social services that people enjoy so much that they consider the tax burden worthwhile. Such a system would allow Americans to "vote with their feet" and locate themselves in a state that governs in the way they find most appropriate. Unfortunately, in today's America, where the federal government exerts complete control in almost every area, there is very little room for states to distinguish themselves from each other, and that results in a lack of choice for every American.

The fact is, the federal powers enumerated in the Constitution are extremely limited in scope, and deal primarily with the way the states interact with each other, and the way that the nation interacts with other nations; a huge departure from the situation we have today, where the federal government dictates to both states and individuals a laundry list of things related to everyday life. According to the enumerated powers in the Constitution, most of the Executive branch should be abolished, with the exception of the original Cabinet departments (Defense, Treasury, State, and Justice). With the abolition of much of the executive department should come the dismantling of the regulatory apparatus. According to the Constitution, the Congress has the power to regulate interstate commerce, but no authority whatsoever to regulate what goes on inside a particular state. The states should be left to decide for themselves the best way to deal with environmental regulation, land use, labor, health care, social services, or any of the other thousand things that the federal government currently dictates. Furthermore, in cases where the state chooses not to regulate, the individual retains full liberty.

*Repeal the 16th Amendment.* The 16th Amendment established the federal government's ability to levy an individual income tax on Americans. The current tax structure is so complex that very few people in the United States actually understand it, and most of those who do work for the government. In addition to being too complex for the average American to understand, the tax code is immoral in two respects. First, it is used to subsidize some behaviors and punish others, through the use of exemptions. The Federal government should not be involved in influencing the personal choices of individual Americans. Second, the entire idea of a tax on income punishes productivity and success, and the current progressive tax structure, where Americans pay a larger percentage of their income as that income increases, only compounds the problem. Supporters of the current tax structure say that the federal government needs the funds that it currently receives from income taxes, and more, and it is only fair that the rich pay more. These statements are false; if the federal government followed its enumerated powers, federal expenditures could easily be cut by 75%, eliminating the need for a federal income tax imposed on individuals. With most of the requirements of day-to-day governance being returned to the states, individual states would be responsible for determining the best way of meeting operating expenses.

*Repeal the 17th Amendment.* When the Constitution was drafted, the bicameral legislature was created in order to give representation in the legislature to both individuals, through the House of Representatives, and to the states, through the Senate. The appointment of senators by state legislatures was an important check on federal power, because senators had to consult regularly with their counterparts in the state legislature, and had to follow their wishes.

The argument for direct election was that it would make senators more directly answerable to the citizens at large. While this sounds good at surface level, a quick analysis of the facts reveals that it is not true. Take, for example, California, the nation's most populous state. The population of California was just over 37 million in 2010. This means that, in order to represent the people, Senators Dianne Feinstein and Barbara Boxer would have to be aware of the wishes of tens of millions of California voters. This, of course, is absurd. Even if both senators desperately wanted to consult with and understand the desires of their constituents (unlikely in our current cynical political system), they would have to attend 74,000 separate 500-person town hall style meetings in order to have an intimate get-together with every person they supposedly represent. Instead, the sheer number of constituents, combined with a political climate that favors incumbency over challengers, means that senators, particularly in high-population states like California, effectively answer to no one, with the possible exception of the corporate interests that finance their reelection campaigns. Instead of making the Senate more answerable to the people, direct election has diluted any effect an individual really has on a senator's livelihood. Selection of senators by legislature makes those senators directly answerable to a small group of legislators, who are each in turn answerable to a smaller constituency. Therefore, repeal of the 17th Amendment and a return to the original framer's intent has the dual benefit of both providing a state check on federal power and making members of the Senate more accountable.

*Return to Constitutional Roles.* Throughout this work, there have been two shifts in power highlighted. First is the shift from state to federal supremacy, which began almost as soon as the Constitution was ratified, and saw its apex at the end of the civil war. The second shift, which began in earnest during the Progressive Era, was the movement from legislative to executive authority. According to the Constitution, it is the job of the legislature to make laws, and the job of the executive branch to enforce them. Article 1, Section 1 of the Constitution reads: "All legislative Powers herein granted shall be vested in a Congress of the United States, which shall consist of a Senate and House of Representatives."

Unfortunately, as was seen during the Progressive Era, the federal government increasingly sought to exert influence over that which had previously been within the control of the individual citizen. As federal control expanded, it became less and less possible for legislators, who rarely had expertise in anything other than government, to write legislation related to the technical disciplines now being regulated. The solution for this was to cede legislative authority to the executive branch by making broad rules and allowing executive bureaucracies to draft the specific regulations that Americans would be bound to.

There are a number of problems that this practice has led to. First, and most simply, the practice itself is illegal. The executive branch of the federal government is tasked with enforcing the law, not making it. This is actually a fairly simple concept. The writers of the Constitution intended for Congress to make the rules, and for the President to enforce them. This was done for a reason, as the founders had witnessed the unchecked authority of a monarch, and did not wish to see it repeated in America. Now, it is possible, two and a quarter centuries later, to change this arrangement through the amendment process, but until that occurs, the hundred-thousand pages plus of bureaucratic regulations that currently oppress the American citizenry are, in fact, illegal.

Second, the practice of administrative rule-making has moved the center of power away from accountability. When it was the legislature that made the rules, the rule-makers were directly answerable to their constituents. In the House of Representatives, this meant the people, and in the Senate, this meant state governments. Any out of control legislation could mean the end of a political career for those who voted for it. Now, with rule-making authority being managed by bureaucrats, there is effectively no accountability, because those who make the rules are not up for reelection. This insulates the petty tyrants in the regulatory apparatus from both the effects of their policies and the understandable anger of those who must live under it. To get an idea of how the executive branch now works, Imagine, for example, that police officers, who are currently tasked with enforcing the law, and are not directly answerable to the public, were also given the authority to draft rules based on broadly-worded guidelines from the elected city council. Effectively, a police officer who had a grudge against a particular citizen could interpret that broad guideline in a way that would make said citizen's actions illegal, and then arrest the citizen on the spot. To most people, this situation is a fairly obvious tyranny. How, then, is the executive branch of the government any different? The executive branch, according to the Constitution, is the federal government's police force. Giving them the authority to create the law set the United States up to be a tyrannical police state, a situation that becomes closer and closer to reality with each subsequent administration.

*Abandon the entitlement state.* Of everything on this list, the abandonment of entitlement spending may be the most difficult sell to the American people. Americans are by and large good people, and it is easy to see entitlement spending as caring for those in need, particularly when politicians and a complicit media use the pitiful specter of starving old crippled people as a political club come election season. Americans, as a result of their compassion, are easily tricked into equating the elimination of entitlements with a vision of the starving poor littering the city streets. Truthfully, however, it is that same compassion that would guarantee that the truly needy never go without, regardless of whether or not the federal government is involved. A return to state and private charity would almost certainly run more efficiently that the schemes currently operating at the federal level, and would have a much better likelihood of making sure that those receiving benefits actually need them.

There is another obstacle that must be overcome, and this one is less virtuous than the compassion that gets exploited in the name of caring for the poor. That obstacle is the sense of individual entitlement that has crept into the American psyche. In order to eliminate the entitlement programs that will, if left unchecked, lead to American bankruptcy, Americans will have to come to terms with the fact that if they wish to retire, they will have to plan and save for it themselves, or rely on care from family, church, or community. Otherwise, it will be necessary for individuals to work through the twilight years in order to support themselves. This sounds harsh, but we have seen the effects of the state-sponsored alternative, and it is not sustainable for more than a few generations. Furthermore, this has not only proven true in the United States, but in many European countries as well, demonstrating that it is the concept of state-funded retirement, not just America's execution of it, which is unworkable.

The elimination of entitlements at the federal level does not just extend to retirement benefits, either. Disability, unemployment, food stamps; all of it must be eliminated if we are to return to liberty and economic sustainability at the federal level. However, like so many other issues highlighted in this work, there is no constitutional prohibition against having these things at the state level, and with a free-market competition put back in place between the states, there is a distinct possibility that a sustainable solution may be discovered. It has usually been proven that where a demand for something exists (in this case care for the poor, disabled, and elderly), the market finds a solution that both works and is economically viable.

*Abandon the Empire.* America's history, beginning with the expansion west, is heavy with military conquest. This is often an uncomfortable truth for Americans to come to terms with, but much of the land that the United States occupies today was taken by force – some justified, as was the case with the original Revolution; some less so, as was seen with the acquisition of Florida and California. The United States has also used its military might to do great good in the world; ridding the world of the Nazi plague that swept Europe in the last century is one such example.

However, the military buildup during the Cold War, the proxy wars fought on its behalf, such as Vietnam, and the eventual fall of the Soviet Union helped to create in the average American the idea that, as the world's only superpower, the United States had not only the right, but the obligation, to weigh in militarily in every conflict on the globe. It has gotten to the point where many political pundits, particularly those who call themselves conservative, posit military intervention as the first and in many cases only option to any conflict or event that goes against what are perceived as America's interests.

Among the many problems with this viewpoint is the fact that frequent military intervention is not compatible with a nation committed to liberty. Unless military action is undertaken in self-defense, it is intended to compel a particular behavior, and compulsion, as has been discussed previously, is the opposite of liberty.

For an example of this inappropriate use of military force, consider the decade-long occupation of Afghanistan. Immediately following the al-qaeda attacks on the World Trade Center and Pentagon on September 11, 2001, it was determined that the Afghan government, a hard-line Islamist regime, was harboring members of the group responsible for the attacks. After demands to turn the perpetrators over were refused, military action was undertaken in order to capture or kill the terrorists and topple the regime that had given them safe haven. All of these actions fall well within the bounds of self-defense and were well justified.

The problem came into play when the Bush administration insisted on staying in the country following the fall of the Taliban government to rebuild and establish a democracy. In the decade following the initial military victory, very little has been accomplished, and the situation has gotten so bad that the U.S. government has been forced to deal with some of the same members of the government that they fought to oust in order to maintain some semblance of order. The reason for this is simple: it is not possible to force a country to adopt democracy at the point of a gun, particularly when the people in that country don't want it. In the region that Afghanistan occupies, cultural and religious systems are not particularly conducive to individual liberty or democracy, and as a result, attempts to force it have been unsuccessful, and it is very likely that any budding democratic reforms will collapse as soon as the U.S. military presence is gone. When this situation is considered in light of what is being attempted – namely the forceful creation of a governmental system that is supposedly rooted in freedom from compulsion, the fact that it has not worked particularly well should not be a surprise.

On top of being both anti-liberty and counterproductive, the American military machine is extremely expensive. The United States maintains nearly 1,000 military bases on foreign soil, all of which are staffed by officers, soldiers, marines, airmen, and sailors far away from their homeland. In total, the staffing and maintenance of these bases costs $30 billion per year. In addition to these ongoing expenses, the Department of Defense has been granted a budget of $130 billion per year for 'overseas contingencies operations' – the new buzzword for military action and occupation in places like Afghanistan, Iraq, and Libya. Add to this the $30 billion doled out as military and economic aid to other nations, and the expenditures for maintaining the American empire rapidly approach a quarter trillion dollars per year, which represents only about 30% of the Department of Defense's nearly $700 billion annual budget. Returning the American military to its rightful place as a force intended to protect from foreign invasion would go a long way to returning the United States to a sensible economic footing.

These seven changes would represent a dramatic change to the America that currently exists, and would require nearly all Americans to change their view of what the government should do, and what should be the responsibility of the individual citizen. Such changes would not be without hardship; many Americans currently rely on support from the government to meet everyday expenses. Removing the existing support structure would place much more burden on families and communities.

This, however, is exactly what the founders intended. What men like Jefferson and Franklin knew, and what has been demonstrated throughout this work, is that people cannot have both liberty and an all-powerful state. In order to maintain freedom, it is necessary for man to take care of himself and his neighbors.

# Ten

# Concluding Thoughts

*"Educate and inform the whole mass of the people... They are the only sure reliance for the preservation of our liberty."*
Thomas Jefferson

Following his retirement from public life in 1809, President Jefferson returned to Monticello, the home he had begun constructing in 1769 on land inherited from his father located in Albermarle County, Virginia. There, he returned to the true passions of his life, the study of philosophy, science, and agriculture. Jefferson himself was no fan of politics; he had once stated that "I have no ambition to govern men; it is a painful and thankless office." It was his desire for the freedom to pursue his passions without government intervention, and the belief that others should be free to do the same, that had led him to the Continental Congress in 1776, as well as to positions as Secretary of State, Vice President, and President. Following his second term, it was his intent to retire, but not to go silent. In the foyer at Monticello, there were maps of the United States, bones of long-extinct animals taken from various locations in America, busts of political philosophers, and decorations, tools, and weapons from Native American tribes. There were also chairs lined up against the walls, and these were frequently filled with visitors from near and far who came to Monticello hoping to get the opportunity to shake the President's hand, and perhaps exchange a few words with him.

Also in the room, in the place of honor above the fireplace, is a copy of an etching depicting the writing of the Declaration of Independence. The reason for this honored location is not because Jefferson wished to remind his visitors of his important place in history; instead it was there as a reminder of the Declaration's important place in history. It was liberty that the President wished his visitors to remember above all else.

Given the course that American history has taken in the nearly two centuries since his death, it is unlikely that Jefferson would either recognize or condone what the America he helped create has become. The centralization of power, which Jefferson battled fellow founder Alexander Hamilton against, the loss of individual liberties, and the American military machine are all things that Jefferson warned against in his own lifetime. In a very real sense, Jefferson's America no longer exists. Two hundred and thirty-five years of progress has seen America move from a loose confederation of states to a centrally-controlled superpower that is now struggling under the weight of its obligations.

This weight, while not felt on a day-to-day basis by most Americans, is nevertheless a very real danger to the way of life for each and every one of them. All of the war, welfare, and bureaucracy costs significantly more than people realize, and while the 'debt crisis' is often referenced in cable-network new programs, it is clearly not at the forefront of most American's minds. This ignorance, willful or unintentional, is dangerous. A recent news article puts United States obligations (debt plus scheduled spending) at over $33 trillion. The total value of the U.S. stock market fluctuates between $15 and $17 trillion, and the total value of Americans' cash assets is around $6 trillion, meaning that if the federal government confiscated all wealth in the nation, it could not pay the bill. Talk about tax increases (usually under the guise of the 'rich' paying 'their fair share') is nothing but a smokescreen; you cannot outspend the total physical assets of a nation of 300 million and honestly think that you can tax your way out of the situation. The government is too big, the result of trying to be everything for everyone, which of course is an impossible feat.

This work, while not exhaustive in its study of American history, is intended to expose the dangerous road that the United States is headed down, and to demonstrate that said direction is not, as many pundits would have the public believe, only the result of whichever recent Administration or Congress they wish to demonize. It is also intended as a counter-example of the American history which is taught in American school rooms. As it has often been pointed out, history is written by those in power, and since the U.S. government has (contrary to the Constitution) chosen to direct public education from Washington, they get first crack at telling impressionable young people all of the great things that have been accomplished since the nation was founded, and how the founders intended it that way all along. Many, if not most, Americans have no idea that Andrew Jackson was a war criminal, that Polk baited the Mexicans into war so we could take California, and that Lincoln was a racist.

Furthermore, Americans may feel that TSA checkpoints are a bit excessive, but don't recognize that they directly violate the fourth amendment, because they give their government too much credit. The same could be said about the Department of Education, the Department of Energy, or any of the other cabinet departments that did not have a seat at George Washington's table. Americans either naïvely believe that the government on the whole really is there to help them, or they see the waste and corruption, but don't realize that there is another way. Another way does exist, and it lies in the recognition of the freedom, liberty, and individuality of every American.

# Author's Notes

I wrote this book with two purposes in mind. First, I have always wanted to write a book and in so doing perhaps influence others in their thinking. The second purpose (hopefully not as narcissistic) was a desire to truly understand the course of American history and why things are so bad now.

That things are bad I saw as a given. As a frequent traveler, I find the line of American sheep waiting to be physically assaulted by incompetent federal agents at the airport disgusting. As a taxpayer, I find the use of federal funds frequently immoral. As a classical liberal, I find the oppressive regulatory regime deplorable. In truth, while I have a great many good things to say about Americans (charity, kindness, and optimism come to mind), I have a very difficult time coming up with anything good to say about 21st Century America.

So I began to read. I read the founders, such as Jefferson, Hamilton, and Madison. I read Adam Smith and John Locke, who influenced much of what the founders had to say. I read more modern economists, particularly Hayek, who literally wrote the book on how to decline economically. I read Woodrow Wilson, which made me cringe as he attempted (successfully) to sell the American public on the idea that the founder's notions were outdated and that centralized planning and authoritarian government were the new freedom. I read speeches by both Presidents Roosevelt, where they waxed poetic on government control of private industry. I have tried to include a great deal of both primary source material and analysis by those more expert than I am in their fields so that you can see what they had to say. I would also recommend that anyone who reads this book take the time to read the works that I have highlighted here.

Over the course of researching and writing this book, I have become more and more convinced that we are in real trouble, but also that there has never really been a time when America is what it could be. I truly believe that freedom and liberty are not only the greatest moral good, but will produce the greatest economic and social success. It is my sincere hope that this work will at least cause some Americans to question the road we have traveled, and the road we currently find ourselves on. It isn't too late to change course and become the land of freedom and opportunity that we can be. As Hayek states at the end of *The Road to Serfdom,* "If in the first attempt to create a world of free men we have failed, we must try again. The guiding principle that a policy of freedom for the individual is the only truly progressive policy remains as true today as it was in the nineteenth century."

# Bibliography

Railway President Held as Seditionist. (1918, April 28). *The New York Times.*

*The Holy Bible, New International Version.* (1995). Zondervan Publishing.

Basler, R. P. (1953). *The Collected Works of Abraham Lincoln, VIII.* Rutgers University Press.

Carnes, J. E. (1862). *The Slave Power: Its Character, Career, and Probable Designs.* New York, NY: Carleton.

Cole, H. L., & Ohanian, L. E. (2009, February 2). How Government Prolonged the Depression. *Wall Street Journal.*

Conrat, M., & Conrat, R. (1992). *Executive Order 9066: The Internment of 110,000 Japanese Americans.* Los Angeles, CA: UCLA Asian American Studies Center Press.

Denson, J. (2006). *Century of War: Lincoln, Wilson & Roosevelt.* Ludwig von Mises Institute.

Hamilton, A., & Madison, J. (2007). *The Pacificus-Helvidius Debates of 1793-1794: Toward the Completion of the American Founding.* University of Michigan.

Hamilton, A., Madison, J., & Jay, J. (n.d.). *Federalist Papers.* Public Domain.

Hayek, F. (2007). *The Road to Serfdom.* Chicago, IL: Chicago University Press.

Heritage Foundation. (n.d.). *Country Rankings: World & Global Economy Rankings on Economic Freedom.* Retrieved from Heritage Foundation: http://www.heritage.org/index/ranking

Jeffrey, T. P. (2011, September 14). *Authors of Social Security Believed It Was Unconstitutional.* Retrieved from CNS News: http://cnsnews.com/blog/terence-p-jeffrey/authors-social-security-believed-it-was-unconstitutional

Jeffrey, T. P. (2011, June 3). *China Has Divested 97 Percent of Its Holdings in U.S. Treasury Bills.* Retrieved from CNS News: http://cnsnews.com/news/article/china-has-divested-97-percent-its-holdings-us-treasury-bills

Locke, J. (n.d.). *Two Treatises on Government.* Public Domain.

Mises, L. v. (2009). *Socialism: An Economic and Sociological Analysis.* Ludwig von Mises Institute.

Monex International. (1975, June). Monex International presents an exclusive interview with Nobel Laureate Dr. Friedrich A. von Hayek. *Gold & Silver Newsletter*, pp. 1-5.

Paine, T. (n.d.). *Common Sense.* Public Domain.

Pease, T. C., & Randall, J. G. (2010). *The Diary of Orville Hickman Browning V1: 1850-1864.* Kessinger Publishing, LLC.

Polk, J. K. (Performer). (1847, December 7). *Third Annual Message.* United States Capitol, Washington, D.C.

Rand, A. (1996). *Atlas Shrugged - 50th Anniversary Edition.* New American Library.

Reporters Without Borders. (n.d.). *Press Freedom Index 2011/2012.* Retrieved from Reporters Without Borders: http://en.rsf.org/press-freedom-index-2011-2012,1043.html

Rothbard, M. (2006). *Making Economic Sense.* Ludwig von Mises Institute.

Social Security Administration. (n.d.). Retrieved from
        Social Security Online History:
        http://www.ssa.gov/history/hlong1.html
Suddath, C. (2010, October 4). *Why Did World War I Just
        End?* Retrieved from Time World:
        http://www.time.com/time/world/article/0,8599,2
        023140,00.html
*Virginia's Ratification - The U.S. Constitution Online.*
        (n.d.). Retrieved from
        http://www.usconstitution.net/rat_va.html
Wilson, W. (2005). *The New Freedom A Call For the
        Emancipation of the Generous Energies of a
        People.* Public Domain Books.
Yale Law School. (n.d.). Retrieved from Avalon Project:
        http://avalon.law.yale.edu